The Conquering Spirit

First published by Mdumiseni Menze in 2022

Intambiso Projects and Leadership Services
Address: 43 Skaamrosie Road, Protea Valley, Bellville, 7530
Email: intambisopls@gmail.com

© Mdumiseni Menze, 2022

All rights reserved. No part of this book may be reproduced or transmitted in any form or by any means, whether print or electronic or any medium that has yet to be discovered. To request permission to reproduce a portion of the book for any purpose, and for all other inquiries, please contact Mdu Menze at intambisopls@gmail.com.

ISBN 978-1-991220-08-0

Also available as an ebook.

Produced by Staging Post, a division of Jacana Media
Cover photo by Winiwe Nyangule
Cover design by Keitu Reid, Helpmyworld
Editing by Natalie Gillman-Biljon
Proofreading by Megan Mance
Set in Sabon LT Std 10.5/14.5pt
Printed and bound by Creda Communications
Job no. 003900

The Conquering Spirit

Mdumiseni Menze

Contents

Acknowledgements	7
Foreword by book compiler, Damaria Senne	11
Chapter 1: Background doesn't matter, until it does	13
Chapter 2: Pick your battles wisely	19
Chapter 3: Take advantage of opportunities that seem small	23
Chapter 4: Establish a culture of hard work	27
Chapter 5: Use the resources you have to propel you towards your goal	33
Chapter 6: Dream big	39
Chapter 7: Establish a culture of education	45
Chapter 8: Recognise the pursuit of your dreams translates differently in real life	53
Chapter 9: Develop a strong spiritual core	61
Chapter 10: Establish strong supportive relationships	69
Chapter 11: Build a strong healthy body and enjoy the benefits	73
Chapter 12: Recognise that some detours will have meaningful impact	79
Chapter 13: The calling journey begins	85

Chapter 14: Learn from your children	89
Chapter 15: Building a church requires collective effort (the Heart of True Worship International church, a case study)	93
Chapter 16: Build a strong capacity for leadership	101
Chapter 17: Find a mentor who can help you grow	107
Chapter 18: Be brave and take a chance: Travel to expand your horizons	111
Chapter 19: Be an agent of change	121
Chapter 20: Take increasingly bigger steps to prepare for your great endeavour	129
Endorsements	137

Acknowledgements

FIRST AND FOREMOST: I WOULD like to thank my God for who, what and where I am in life because of His grace and love.

Secondly: I would like to take this moment to express my sincere heartfelt gratitude to all those who continue to mould me and contribute in many different ways to my personal growth and development.

Kwikhaya Lakwa Menze: KooSukude, Mkhondwana, Santsaba, Thuwa, Sihula, Thole'lomthwakazi, Gxarheliphezulu, Hlahlelagawulwa Phesheyakomlanjana, Bhalelesendeni, Nxebalisemphakathweni Elingabonwa Ngumfazi, Ithintombi Ndizeke Inkomo Zolandela, Umfazi Obele Linye Phesheya Komlanjana.

Ndiyabulela ngokundinika imvelaphi.

To my Parents: My mother Nopasile Menze, uMakhiwa and my late father Amstrong Kebetu Menze, uMkhondwana for being there for me even before I was born and for raising me with values and principles that have become the bedrock of the man I am today. I appreciate your selfless efforts and hard work to ensure I had food in my stomach, the mealie pap with rooibos tea and sometimes with cabbage: our daily growing up menu. Thank you for believing in me, for seeing something special in me even in those early ages when I was just a dusty-looking boy coming from the veld with cracked feet. You created an environment conducive to nurturing me and allowing me to thrive. Above all, I will forever be grateful to you for exposing my life to God, His Word and Salvation plan. Ndibamba ngazo zozibini. May your soul continue resting in peace my father.

To my siblings: Vuyo, Vuyokazi, Andiswa, Cikizwa, Siphokazi, Zandile, Zikhona, Phelokazi and Osca if I were to say something about each one of you, then the book would have to be all about you bantase. This is not because you are a huge number, but because of who you are, what you have been and continue to be in my life. I specifically want to thank you for covering my nakedness in times that I am naked and for your love and support. I know at times you cannot take the person that I am because we are different but you continue to embrace and love me unconditionally.

To my friends:

Pumezo Myataza: You are the very first person that I could call a friend in life. Thanks, buddy, for your genuine love and patience. You ushered me to all my favourite hobbies, ballroom and Latin American dance, playing pool and table tennis. I'm grateful, mate!

Lulamile Tshongweni: My university friend, the man from Tsakane Township! Your love and inspiration during those varsity years will forever live in my heart. Do thank your family on my behalf for all those freshly baked scones they sent through to us while on campus. They brought so much luxury, joy and comfort while we were busy licking our wounds from tough exams, assignments and tutorials. We dreamed together and saw a distant bright future coming our way; you made varsity life less challenging and more fulfilling.

Delphino Machikicho: My young brother from another mother! You are such a wise and hardworking man. I am grateful for your love, support and for pushing me to the top of the mountain at all times. I am also humbled by your manner of respect and honour.

Lackson Mrevesi: My friend, you always have my best interests at heart. Thank you for being a pure-hearted person and for your willingness to serve. I am always comfortable asking you to do anything at any time for me and you always help. Your love, prayers and support are highly appreciated.

Mandisi Mtyhida: My Pastor, you have played a very important role in my spiritual growth and development. Your consistent presence, love and selfless support in my life will never be taken for granted. Thank you Mayarha.

Pastor Goodman Oyama Zeyise Xabanisa, umshumayeli oxabanisa noSatana! You are like a brother to me. I thoroughly enjoy your hospitable spirit, and your braai meat is the best. Whenever we are sitting enjoying braai meat (sisika inyama) you always manage to say something that stimulates my mind and shifts my perspective. Your joking and laugh-out-loud manner uplifts my spirits. I would like to thank you for your brotherhood.

Ta-Mzo (Mzothando Mtikitiki): My humble, loving and supportive brother who takes my problems and challenges to heart. I appreciate all the time you take to listen to me, then guide and give all the necessary support without being judgemental. Thank you for freely sharing even your professional expertise and services when needed. Hlala unjalo Zotsho.

To my mentors:

Bishop Dunga and his wife Apostle Agnes Dunga: You gave birth to me spiritually and allowed God to use you as instruments of transformation from a hopeless life without Christ into a new everlasting, gracious life of the kingdom of Christ. For that, I am forever grateful.

My spiritual mentor Pastor Mthandeni Vanya and his wife Bongiwe Vanya: You are very valuable gifts in my spiritual journey. Thank you for always praying for me and for just loving me. You have consistently walked with me, supportive of all my efforts since 2009, which is over a decade by now. Ndiyambulela uthixo ngawe Matshaya.

My Leadership Mentor Mr Jannie Isaacs: You are a man of excellence, quality and development. A man who believes in doing the right things, the right way, a great listener and assessor. You have been instrumental in moulding and sharpening my leadership journey, sir, and I am blessed to have met a man of your stature. I love you, sir, long live!

To my wife and sons:

Thank you Dr Ayanda Mfokazi-Menze, Zizikazi: One of the reasons I married you, my wife, besides the love, was I needed someone that would keep me on my toes. Someone that would challenge me. You are very intelligent with clear contents when you speak. You really keep me on my toes, have shaped my thinking and my way of doing things. You have taught me to be clear and solid of the reasons behind my every action and you therefore play an important role in my life. You are a great cook and serve the best dishes. I also appreciate that you are a very hardworking person with a very strong personality yet so loving and a firm believer in love. I thank you Jama Kasjadu for being a very generous giver even to a point of sharing me with the communities and thus allowing me to serve my purpose in my generation.

A special thanks to my sons Nkitha, Ezekiel and Emmanuel: You guys are adorable and very special in different ways. I thank God for blessing me with such incredible human beings. Thank you for sharing me with the communities and thus allowing me to serve my purpose in my generation.

The late Damaria Senne, the book compiler: When we selected you among the best, we had no doubt that you would do a great job. Thank you for interpreting my transcript and making what was a dream a reality. It is such a pity you are not here to witness your project reach completion, as the Lord decided to render you rest. May your beautiful soul continue to rest in peace.

Last but not least, to the person reading this book right now: I would like to thank you for buying my book. I believe you will learn something and be refreshed by it. May God bless you!

Foreword by book compiler, Damaria Senne

As I was working through Mdumiseni's story, I could feel the project transition from being another client project in my schedule to becoming a passion project. I was standing in my kitchen, making myself a cup of tea during one of my breaks when it finally fully registered to me that Mdu had faced enough challenges to break many people. But he had not given up. We can all learn from that.

This book is not just about overcoming hardships; it's a celebration of life. It's about a man who enjoys his life despite the difficulties. And can he laugh and laugh!

Another reason I loved working on this project is that Mdu delves into the minutiae of his background and journey through life. We learn that he was a late admission to his high school and the consequences of that. We know what he did to create the opportunity to pursue tertiary studies in Cape Town.

Through his storytelling, we learn whether the solutions he applied worked or failed, and what alternatives finally worked. And when he does something unwise it eventually bit him; these tiny details are very illuminating.

I hope that the readers of this book will not only be inspired but will also use it as a tool in empowering themselves. This book is not appropriate for a quick scan. The principles and strategies employed here are worth internalising in our psyches and applying in our own lives.

Don't just take my word for it. Please make sure to read the numerous endorsements that are in the last chapter of this book. The people who grew up, studied, worked and lived with Mdu were happy to share their experiences of life with him.

Chapter One
Background doesn't matter, until it does

LET ME TELL YOU ABOUT my ancestral family to give you context of where I come from; because I believe that the actions of the people in my lineage influenced the structure of the family I was born into and the man I would grow up to become.

The Menze family: OoSukude, Mkhondwana, Thuwa, Santsaba, Sihula, Thole'lomthwakazi, Gxarheliphezulu, Hlahlelagawulwa Phesheya Komlanjana, Bhalelesendeni, Nxebalisemphakathweni Elingabonwa Ngumfazi, Ithintombi Ndizeke Inkomo Zolandela, Umfazi Obele Linye Phesheya Komlanjana; have their ancestral roots originating from Nqgeleni, Kunomadolo location kwaThuwa. The community is named after our clan name because our clan dominates the village. Nqgeleni is a small rural town within the Eastern Cape Province of Southern Africa, 33.9km from Mthatha. Kunomadolo was and still is a naturally beautiful rural village carpeted with green grass and vegetation, decorated by lots of trees and shrubs because it is blessed with a rich black soil where livestock also thrives.

Now come, let's trace my lineage starting with Mkhosana, my great-great-grandfather. Mkhosana gave birth to two sons, Menze the elder son and Mbhayibhayi. Menze, had two sons Sihoyo the older son and Bambiso the younger son. Sihoyo made a contribution of five sons into the family: Lufele, Bobo, Masayina, Nombinana and Tshodela.

Bambiso gave birth to three sons: Noyila, Mngeni and Nomkwaqulo.

Are you starting to feel like you're reading Genesis in the Bible and having a hard time keeping track of who begat whom? Check out my family organogram below for visual clarification.

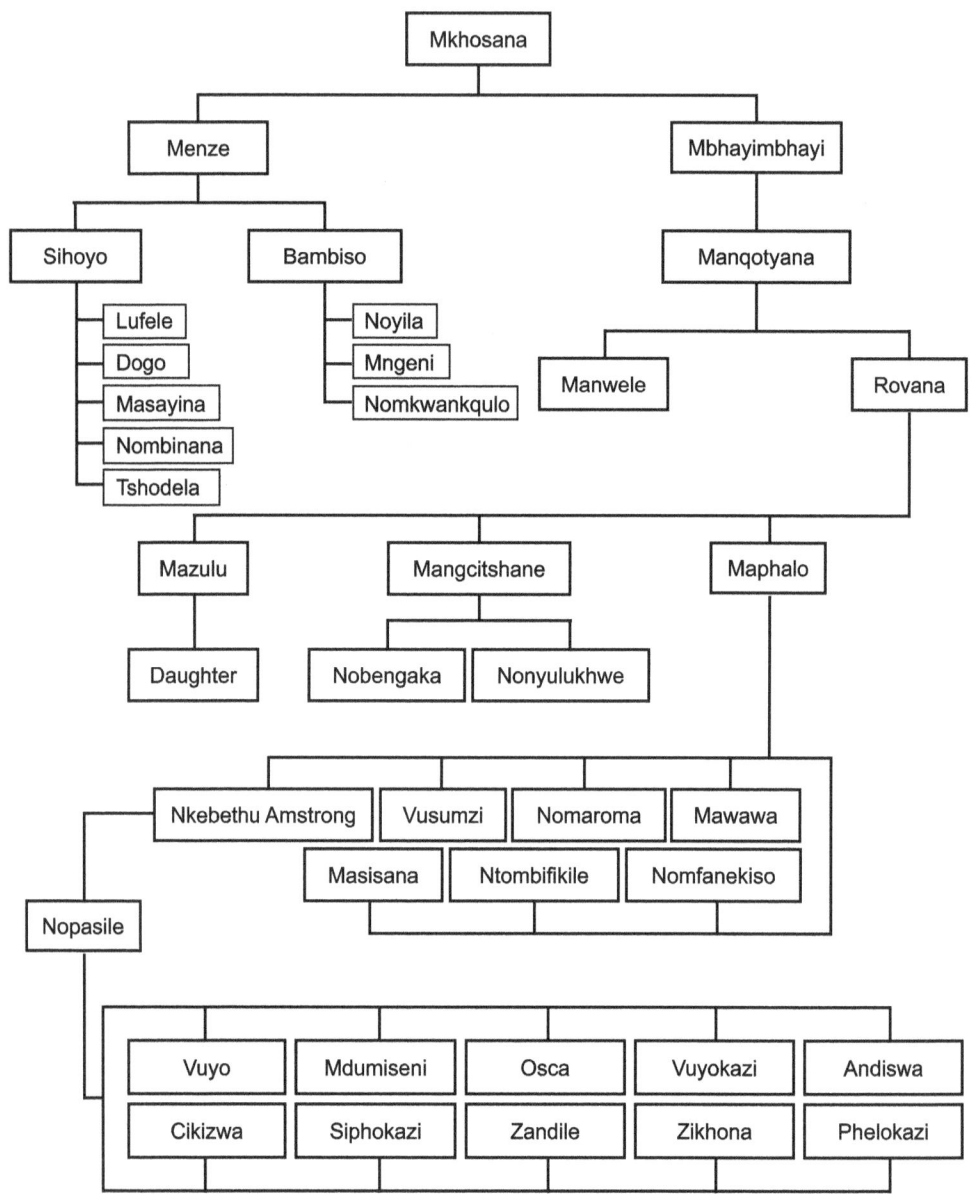

Table 1: The Menze family organogram

As you can see, Mbhayimbayi gave birth to one son, Manqotyana. Manqotyana gave birth to two sons, Manwele and Rovana. My grandfather Rovana was a strong man who died at the advanced age of 94. He had three wives. His great wife was Mazulu, who gave birth to one daughter. They have both passed away. The middle wife, Mangcitshane, gave birth to two children: Nobengaka, a son, and Nonyulukhwe, a daughter. They have also both passed away.

The young wife, Bhabha, Umaphalo, gave birth to seven children: the two sons were the late Kebetu, uAmstrong and Vusumzi, and the five daughters are the late Nomaroma, Mawawa, Masisana, Ntombifikile and Nomfanekiso. Maphalo is in her nineties and still kicking strong, left with four children: one son and three daughters.

My father, Nkebethu, married Nopasile Menze nee Mgayo uMakhiwa. Together they made a huge contribution into society of ten children. Their three sons are Vuyo, Mdumiseni and Osca and their seven daughters are Vuyokazi, Andiswa, Cikizwa, Siphokazi, Zandile, Zikhona and Phelokazi. I see it as a blessing to have such amazing siblings; they are all special in different ways. They are not perfect. However, in their imperfection, they continue to do great things and play a pivotal role in my life.

My father was a strong leader and a man full of wisdom. He began working at a mine in Gauteng before joining the former South African Iron and Steel Industrial Corporation (Iscor), now known as Arcelor Mittal South Africa after being acquired by Ispat International NV, to work as a labourer.

During the period my father worked for Iscor, Apartheid was still going strong in South Africa and, as a result, people landed jobs and promotions based on their race, or, if you were Black, based on your complexion.

Based on the above criteria, the company was delighted to offer him a position as a foreman because he had lighter skin than the average Black person in South Africa. However, he had never set foot in a schooling environment, and his lack of education nixed the possibility of a promotion. He believed that education would bring people like him and his family a great many opportunities. He was saddened by the fact that he had missed out on getting an education. The thing is, his parents were also uneducated, so they didn't quite understand the benefits thereof.

"If I was educated, I would be in parliament," he would always say.

That wish was ultimately fulfilled when the South African government began to offer Adult Basic Education classes and he was able to register. However, since he had always thought highly of himself, he measured his capabilities and decided that Grade 4 classes were appropriate for a beginner of his stature.

Unfortunately for my daddy dearest, he had not considered the fact that he would be operating in unfamiliar territory, with tools he could not handle. Learning difficulties were inevitable. But, he was so determined to succeed that he refused demotion; we are talking here about a man who had a reputation to protect at all costs. He said that on his first day in class, they asked him questions that were obviously suitable for Grade 4 learners and he was unable to answer any of them. He said things got worse when they gave him mathematical problems, which induced instant severe headaches. He said from that day on he respected education. He said he thought of answers until he felt blank as he did not know where to start; it felt close to cracking his skull, basically. He said he had a blackout that day he would never forget as it showed him flames.

My mother also never attended school while growing up. She spent her days looking after her father's livestock. We can now qualify her as a shepherdess.

THINGS FOR YOU TO THINK ABOUT:

1. Do you believe that your clan, family and grandparents have a significant impact on your chances of success? Why do they have impact/not have any impact?
2. If you believe that they have an impact, what role do you see them playing in you developing a conquering spirit?
3. Study your lineage – who are your ancestors? Do you know your grandparents, their parents and grandparents?
4. If you have little information about your family and ancestors, is there someone in your community you can ask? If you hit a dead-end, gather as much information about your immediate family as possible.

5. Make a note of important factors that influenced your family and ancestors: culture, religion, common interests, their sphere of work and where they lived.
6. What did your family, grandparents and ancestors need to live well?
7. Write down any significant traits in your lineage. For example, was your grandfather a good businessman or a great teacher?
8. Does your current environment nurture these traits?
9. Do you want to follow in their footsteps, or do you want to chart your own path, in ways that your family never explored?

Chapter Two

Pick your battles wisely

ONE YEAR, WHILE MY FATHER was visiting his family in Nqgeleni from work at the mines. His father told him he must get married. My grandfather continued to ask if he had found a young woman to wed yet, and he said no. One of my father's older sisters said, "I saw a girl who would suit you very well. It's George's daughter."

"I don't want her. She has small legs," he said.

"She is not going to play football!" my grandfather pointed out.

It happened that my grandfather knew George Mgayo and considered him a good man. The Mgayo family is from Mgojweni, a community that is in close proximity to Kunomadolo. He accepted the daughter as a potential daughter-in-law even though he had never met her. He was confident that, as George's daughter, she was likely to become the perfect wife for my father.

"George is a good man, and I expect him to have good daughters," he said. In the olden days the family where the wife comes from was important to determine whether the wife would be a good one or not based on how her family behaves. If the family was deemed good, then their daughters were deemed good for marriage. Hence my grandfather's recommendations for my father's wife.

So the decision was finalised that my father would marry George's daughter, whether he wanted to or not. They said that if he still did not want her after living with her as husband and wife, they would accept the situation and he could pay lobola for another young woman of his choice. But he must know that George's daughter would remain his wife. This was one of the ways that customary marriages were preserved.

My grandfather facilitated the marriage while my father went back to work at the mines. Just like my father, my mother was unable to reject the marriage. She was also from a very traditional rural Xhosa family and followed the traditions and customs of her people. These included agreeing to an arranged marriage with my father.

On several occasions, when my father would come back to visit the family from his mine job, his father would instruct him to go and fetch his wife. My father would obey. He would usually say at all those times, he did not feel like fetching this woman who was supposed to be his wife, and would wish death on himself. He said he felt hurt being forced into the arrangement. But he knew he did not have a choice, as he could not put up his will against his father and against generations of tradition and expect to win.

It turned out that the family choice was spot-on and George's daughter was a perfect wife for him as he never opted to marry a second wife of his choice. They managed to raise ten children together and remained happily married from 1975 until his death on 1 April 2017 due to a tragic car accident.

The way my grandfather convinced my father to marry my mother is a story that became a family legend. Another story that is a family legend is when my mother was three months pregnant with me, my father predicted that the baby would be a boy. The boy was to be named Mdumiseni uYehova uYesu ulithemba labakholwayo, which in English means He Will Praise the Lord and Jesus is the Hope of Those Who Believe.

There were no ultrasound scans in rural hospitals to reveal the gender of the expected bundle of joy. But, as it happened, the baby was a boy and as per my father's wishes, I was named Mdumiseni. My mother gave me a second name of Siyabonga. My parents decided that the second name would be used as my school name. There was a trend then where learners were given school names, besides the birth name, and then an English name. Many people ended up having three names: the birth name, school name and the English name. My father also nicknamed me David, influenced by the Word of God. Later on in life when I received Jesus Christ I was given another name, Daniel, which also comes from the Bible because of the gift of faith. That leaves me with a grand total of four names: Mdumiseni, Siyabonga, David, Daniel Menze, although I am popularly known as Mdu. I am well decorated with names.

***

I was born at a time when my father was predominantly spending his life working in Johannesburg at Iscor. As a result, I did not spend a lot of time with him. When I was around eight months old, I became very sick.

The family took me to a doctor in Libode. Evidently, I was crying 24/7. My mother and grandmother tried as many solutions as they could find. They even walked 17.4km from Mthatha, at night, to take me to an intercessor to pray for me. I did not get better even after the intercessory prayer.

Eventually, they took me to Johannesburg, which is 893.9km from Nomadolo. That was a serious trip for an ill village baby.

When my father saw that I was sick and helpless, he immediately prayed to God and expressed himself this way: "Dear God, I really needed a second boy, but I did not want a sick one. So if you have decided to give me a sick one, then please take him back." Soon after, I began to get better. My father was unaware then that he had in actual fact dedicated and given my life to the Lord.

While I remained in Gauteng, I would be fine health-wise, but as soon as we went back home to the Eastern Cape, the illness would resume. As a result, my mother moved with me to Sebokeng township in Gauteng. That was the year that my younger sister was born. I got better while we stayed in Sebokeng. It seemed city life solidified the state of my health. I must have been a naughty child who craved city life and my father's love. I probably felt that the village life was not suitable for me.

***

Eventually, we needed to go back home to the Eastern Cape; by that time, my family believed that the source of my health problems was a spiritual attack from my father's family. So, they took me to live with my maternal family. Granny Mabhedla, who is still alive, always makes sure to lay claim to me as her son. She loved me so much that she did not want to give me back to my parents when they were ready to take me back later on. My father insisted that I should go back to my homestead because if I did not return I might be deprived of an opportunity to get an education. Remember, my mother's community still remained way behind as far as education was concerned. My father feared that if I spent any more time there I would spend my life working as a shepherd.

THINGS FOR YOU TO THINK ABOUT:

1. Were there any difficulties in your childhood that your parents encountered?
2. Write down how your parents resolved each problem, if they did.
3. As a child, were you empowered by watching your parents face their challenges or, in hindsight, did it leave you with the feeling of being helpless because "life is unfair"?
4. What lessons did you take from that experience?
5. In your view, do you believe that my father gave in on an issue that would define his life?
6. If you were – like him – faced with an important battle that you did not believe you could win, what would you do? Or if this has happened to you (not the specific arranged marriage issue, but something similar), what was your strategy? Did you wade into battle because the situation was unfair, adopt a wait-and-see attitude or simply give up, believing "life's unfair"?
7. What was the outcome of your battle?
8. Would you repeat this strategy again if you were faced with a similar battle, where it looks like you can't win?
9. What did you learn from the experience of facing this type of situation?

Chapter Three
Take advantage of opportunities that seem small

IN 1985, MY FATHER made a tough decision and took a bold step to uproot his family from its roots in Ngqeleni all the way to Qumbu, Mthozela, Tembisa location still, within the Eastern Cape. Qumbu is a small rural town along the N2 towards Durban. The reason for the move was to boost our livestock farming prospects because the village was said to have even more endless, richer and greener pastures than kuNomadolo, which were ideal for farming. Mthozela does have big open fields with a big forest, and lots of summer rains but also very cold winter seasons.

I began my schooling in that village, firstly at Qgili Primary School. Unlike my father who began in grade 4, I did not skip Sub Small A, which would be equivalent to Grade 1 nowadays. I followed this up with a move to Chokomfeni Junior Secondary School, where I completed my primary school and junior education level. My entrepreneurship journey began with a forced one: I used to sell snacks for my mother at school.

I hated selling snacks and sweets but I did not have a choice, as my mother would punish me harshly. It was embarrassing to sell snacks as a boy at school, as my peers viewed me as one with no timing, ibari. There were days that I asked girls who were my friends to sell on my behalf because other boys would make fun of me, calling me weak. I guess such experiences count as one of the things that played a role in my mental strength development, being in a situation where you are forced to do something that you do not want to do. It was the parent's way. End of story.

The school had seasonal activities: soccer, running and school choir. Everyone, including me, avoided running as a sport because we did not see it as interesting. Now I wonder what would have happened if I had started running then. I might have represented the province, even the country, because now that I am a runner, I can see that I have an inherent talent for running.

The soccer team was strong – becoming part of the team was at premium pricing. So I was never selected to join them. However, one day at a school sports tournament, my school team won the right to play early in the morning. They were scheduled to play the first game. The game venue was at least 7km from our school and we had to walk the distance.

The rules were that if a soccer team was late and the challengers were present, the team would play two sides. Some members of our soccer team were delayed that day, and unless a miracle happened, we would default the game.

I was early, so our players asked that my friends and I join them to fill the empty spots. As I was a goalkeeper for my community soccer team, it is the position I chose. The co-opted players did not have a soccer kit but we played well. I even managed to block a penalty kick. The challengers won the game but not without a battle from us, as we tied with them by the designated end time, and were granted extra time. We went on into the penalties where we lost the game.

This game remains memorable to me because it granted me an opportunity to do something I always wanted to do. I didn't get into the team but the knowledge that I played well, without training, at something I was not perceived to be good at, boosted my confidence to try new things.

Besides school sports and cultural activities, we played indigenous games at school. One of those games was fighting with sticks made with paper or grass. We wrapped the homemade stick (called imibhumbhutho) with plastic. Some of the players inserted stones inside the paper or grass stick. The stoned sticks gave heavy blows and caused players to bleed.

We created teams based on communities where we lived. After

writing winter June exams, we would go to the nearby mountain, group ourselves and start hitting each other. There were days when some players hid wood sticks near the play area. They got them in the heat of the game and hit their opponents with them. We then had to run away because we were unevenly matched. Sometimes, it happened that they caught one of our team members and we would have to go back for a rescue mission. Rescue strategy involved stronger players putting themselves in the line of fire until someone could drag the casualty to safety. We played this game from Grade 3 (Standard 1 then) until Grade 9 (Standard 7).

Hierarchy was also important to young boys in our time. During winter seasons, we usually stood against the class walls facing the sun in order to warm ourselves up. We fought over who had better access to the sunshine. We considered it a sign of disrespect to stand in front of someone, blocking their access to the sun.

The sun situation taught me that those who were considered stronger expected to have better access to prime resources. But they also had to fight to keep their position because there was never a day without challengers.

However, selling sweets for my mother at school taught me that there was a higher rank in our society than even the highest-ranking boy in school. The boys may have laughed at me because they said selling sweets was weak but I knew there was a greater authority in my life whose word superseded theirs. I was not aware of it at the time, but selling snacks and sweets at school also taught me that some people will laugh at me if I run a business that they view as beneath me, or that injures my standing in their eyes. However, my persistence helped me support my mother to provide for our family, which was a great outcome.

I learned from stick-fighting that some people will lie and manipulate the situation to their advantage. Having said that, I also learned that sometimes the strong protect the weak, making sure they are all in good health to fight another day.

The biggest lesson I took from these experiences is that life is full of challenges but we can choose how we approach them. Seemingly small opportunities may bring us small rewards, like the internal changes playing in our school soccer team fostered in me; or they may have meaningful impact, like the realisation that selling sweets and snacks at school was a viable business that sustained my family.

THINGS FOR YOU TO THINK ABOUT:

1. What did you want badly while you were in primary school?
2. Did you get it? Explain what you think the reasons are.
3. Did you feel that your talents while you were a child were appreciated by the people around you, or were they underestimated?
4. What was that talent/venture you wanted to do?
5. What was your response? Did you decide to live up to people's expectations of you? Or did you decide to work hard to succeed despite the lack of support?
6. What are the small opportunities that you remember grabbing in your life?
7. Did you take them all up, or did you pass on some of them because you did not believe they would have a meaningful impact on your life?
8. What was the outcome of you accepting those opportunities?
9. What was the outcome of you passing on those opportunities?
10. Looking back now, would you change your response to those small opportunities? Why?

Chapter Four
Establish a culture of hard work

IN MY FAMILY THERE were no girl- or boy-chores. Everyone did every job that needed doing, from grinding maize with a stone, to preparing meals such as porridge, pap and samp. We all flattened and cleaned our house floors with cow dung and collected wood and water, which we carried on top of our heads.

I still have a scar on the fourth finger of my left hand from an accident that happened while I was doing chores. On the way home from the river with my older sister, the bucket fell and, while I was trying to grab it, it injured my finger, making a gaping cut. My sister was unable to assist me during the incident because it happened within the twinkling of an eye. While my family was empathetic towards me for the injury, they were also philosophical about it: in life, stuff happens and we do our best to carry on nonetheless.

Another of my regular chores was looking after my father's livestock, which included cattle and sheep. We could not leave them to graze unattended during the sowing season, because many community members planted maize then and our livestock could destroy their fields. One day we left them and they went into a neighbour's maize farm and destroyed it. My father was heavily fined for that fiasco.

We could not leave the livestock alone during the rainy season either, because they could get lost due to bad weather. I spent a long time in the forest minding the livestock until it was time to take them home. Then I locked them up in the kraal.

Working with animals was fraught with risk. For example, my job involved training horses to be ridden and cows to be yoked. Some cows did not adapt well to a yoke of slavery and would fight very aggressively for their freedom, I suppose. We yoked cows so that we could use them as a form of transportation to collect wood from the forest in a wagon for home delivery.

We also trained horses to familiarise them with the idea of having human beings riding on them. They were just as likely to throw off the trainer as they would allow the same trainer to stay on, a 50/50 kind of win or lose situation. Some of the trainers ended up with cracked limbs because horses threw them off or kicked them.

I also fell a couple of times from a horse during its training. One time, it dropped me off on a gravel road, and I lost consciousness. Eventually that horse became very obedient, and anyone could ride him without issues.

We also used horses to visit nearby communities that were within a 5km radius of our village. These were not impulsive trips, they were scheduled and well-prepared for, as there was a risk that boys from other villages would attack us. We had to be ready to climb on a horse and run for our lives if we were under attack.

Collecting wood from the forest involved a process of hunting and identifying a tree that was made of good wood. It's not as easy and as simple as just chopping down any random tree. Being in the forest also exposed us to a range of wild animals that posed danger to us. Many times when I came across snakes in the forest I simply ran away. My big brother's advice about my snake cowardice was that the only way I would stop seeing snakes was by beating them.

One day I saw a snake crossing the path in front of us.

"Don't run," my brother cautioned me. "If you do, you will see it again."

We attacked it together and, when it was dead, he said, "You see, now that you won against a snake you will not see them often."

I'm still not sure whether this was the truth or a myth but it seemed to have worked for a while. Well, until I lost my hunting dog to a snake bite. I loved that dog and his death was a great sadness and loss to me. My brother and I were in the forest directing our livestock home when we came across the snake.

My brother saw it first and instructed, "Stop the cows!"

When my dog saw the snake, he attacked. He lost the fight, as he was not experienced at fighting snakes. There was a belief in my community that after a snake bites an animal, it must be quickly taken to the river to drink water before the snake gets to drink water first. This would supposedly dilute the strength of the venom in the animal's body. Whoever gets to drink water first between the animal and the snake would dissipate the effects of the venom. I could not grab my dog and run to the nearest river, as it was very dangerous for a person to run into that particularly sloppy riverbed when the snake was also within that vicinity. So, I sadly lost the race and he died. I never had a dog after that incident. I suspect I never really recovered from the trauma of losing him. I may also just not have had the opportunity to get one.

Incidentally, should it happen that a snake bites a human being, so the myth goes, the person shall not cross the river, should one cross the venom will be strengthened. The person shall avoid any path that involves crossing rivers at all cost.

* * *

There was a specific routine to managing our household chores, creating a steady predictability to our days and weeks, which made the lives of ten siblings much simpler. For example, on weekends we did our laundry at the river. The laundry included my parents' and siblings' clothes. As you can imagine, doing girls' and women's laundry was fraught among the other boys who would randomly pay a visit at the river and laugh at me for touching, and actually washing, women's clothes. So I had to do those clothes quickly and thoroughly before the other boys came. When they came I hid them and waited for the boys to leave before resuming washing the clothes. I found it embarrassing to wash women's clothes, especially because the boys said I was going to be soft. However, I ignored them because my mother had a greater influence on me than they did.

I also used to make a lot of tea for my mother. She did not sleep well if she didn't receive a cuppa just before bed. The habit became so ingrained in me that sometimes I made sure to wait for her to come home first when she had gone out before I could go to bed.

Some days when my mother would make it home very late, my siblings would go to sleep while I waited alone. I was obsessive about fulfilling this task and would not sleep.

When my siblings and I had completed one task, we were then expected to find something else that was next on the to-do list. This went on until the sun went to sleep in the evening. Then the family would sit around the fire and enjoy each other's company until we began to feel sleepy. This was a moment of family bonding although at that time we did not understand its significance. To us, it was simply family time.

In case you're starting to wonder if my growing years were a depressing, hard slog, let me disabuse you of that notion. There were plenty of moments where I played games with my sisters. We played three tins, jump rope and hide-and-seek.

Working together as a family team helped us to form a strong bond. We have grown to understand, know and appreciate each other's strengths and weaknesses well into adulthood. Working hard together on a project is an effective way to build a team, and it leaves all the team members with a euphoric sense of accomplishment once the job is done.

I also learned to appreciate being conscientious when doing a task, and the consequences of trying to cut corners. Remember that time when I left the livestock unattended? It seemed like a small matter when I did it but many people paid for that action. Our neighbours lost their maize crops, putting their main food source for the year at risk. My actions reflected badly on my parents according to the village elders, so I damaged their reputation. My family also suffered financial loss because of the fine my father had to pay. I also created a stressful situation for my mother and siblings, due to my father's anger and the threat that we would all get a hiding from him.

Developing a culture of hard work also involves making a second or even tenth attempt, if you fail at a task. For example, I had to get back on a horse after it threw me off. And the boys who were thrown and kicked by their horses? Once they recovered, they were back at it, working with the horses all over again.

I learned that developing a routine can help me manage my work and I have taken that into my adult working environment, where I have many roles to fulfil. Once I complete a task, I don't have to waste time wondering what comes next because I can immediately move on to whatever is next on the to-do list.

A culture of hard work also translates to doing and completing the task at hand, because unfinished work can never be counted as done. Sometimes if I left a job incomplete, half-done or sloppy, I would often find that the following day the job had been complicated somehow or the results were not as gratifying. For example, I knew that if I picked any piece of wood for our fire that was thick, it took too long to catch fire, while thin branches burned-up too fast and tree branches that were too fresh and still wet inside created too much smoke.

THINGS FOR YOU TO THINK ABOUT:

1. Did you have chores assigned to you by your parents when you were growing up?
2. What were those chores?
3. Which chores were more challenging? Which chores did you enjoy doing?
4. What did you learn from the chores now when you look back?
5. Which chores are you still doing?
6. Do you agree or disagree that children should take part in doing household chores? What are your reasons for your standpoint?
7. Have you ever had to do a task even when you were tired and just wanted to sit down and rest? What did you do?
8. What was the outcome?
9. Which of the following strategies do you believe is more likely to enhance your work ethic when you are asked to do a task while you are tired, sleepy or just don't want to do it?
    a) Quietly do the task anyway.
    b) Quit the task because you feel like a slave.
    c) Do the task slowly while taking rest to manage your energy levels.

    d) Do the task while complaining bitterly about the unfairness of the situation.
    e) Do the task badly to punish the person insisting you do it, so that they never mistake you for a doormat again?
10. Which of the above strategies have you ever employed in your life? (Please note, I'm not asking which strategy is most effective or "right". This is about what you believe.) What was the outcome? Would you use the strategy again?
11. Have you ever worked badly with a team? How did you feel when the task was completed?
12. Have you ever worked well with a team? How did you feel when the job was accomplished?

Chapter Five

Use the resources you have to propel you towards your goal

IN THE VILLAGE, WE HAD a wide range of fun activities that kept us entertained, including pottery such as sculpting clay cows, horses and cars. We also dived into engineering crafts, designing wire cars, hunting rats and birds using spring-based traps or wood plug mechanisms to catch the rats. Birds were tougher to catch compared to the rats, because we could simply put in place our rat-catching mechanisms on their predictable pathways, which were so obviously visible against the lush green grass. Actually, my motivation to enrol for mechanical engineering later on in life was inspired by the wire cars. I was great at making wire cars, though they were not very strong as I was more concerned about the beauty than the strength.

Some of my hunting mates could catch between 30 and 100 rats, depending on the status of traffic on rodent pathways. Of course you're probably curious to know what we did with these rats. Well, I didn't eat them! But I participated in the hunt as a way to hang out with my friends and then gave my catch away to them for a braai. My friends used some of the rats as part of medical practice. For example, if someone had bed-wetting issues, the prescription would be to eat a rat of a specific breed identified by its three lines on the back.

As previously mentioned, it was harder to catch birds. Sometimes we spent a full day on the mountains without a single catch. Desperate measures were to try and hit them with a stick, which required skilful precision aiming at moving targets.

At times we came back from our hunting trips empty-handed. One day our consolation prize was catching an owl, which was believed to be an "evil" bird and therefore not edible. But when we caught it, we hosted a braai right there in the forest and swam in the river as a celebration. The braaied owl smelled so good that I planned to eat some of it despite my family warning me against it. But my brother arrived at that moment of my consideration. I had to abandon my possible feast but my friends ate it all. Hunting a deer was the worst proposition compared to bird hunting, as they were scarce in our area. We also needed very fast dogs to secure a successful catch. As an alternative to a deer, we caught plenty of rabbits. During our hunts, we met boys from other villages and competed with them through our rabbit-hunting endeavours.

Our dogs were very sharp. We used to dry snake heads and dead spiders in the sun. Once they dried out, we would then grind them with a stone and incorporate the resultant powder into the dog food. We believed this concoction made our dogs very brave and virulent and would evoke a furious and dangerous spirit within them.

The bad part about this was when the dog attacked a person, that poison was part of the dog's saliva and infected the wound, making it harder for it to heal. We used traditional medicine to heal those wounds. I was once at the receiving end of this mysterious, mystical and mythical practice. I went to one of the community houses for an errand. At my arrival, the dogs started barking and the owner of the dogs did not have a stick to stop them. He asked to use mine because he knew that if I stopped them myself, that would transfer his authority over them to me. I made a mistake and gave him my stick. The dogs attacked me and bit me. I still have a scar from that wound on my right leg.

While minding the livestock, we used fights to create a hierarchy among ourselves. Losers in the fights became the skivvy of the group. The boys that won the fights had the privilege of demanding honourable service from the other boys.

Also, whenever a new boy visited a particular village, upon arrival the village boys organised him a fighting match against the reigning community champion. If the new boy defeated and claimed the champion belt, he was immediately respected by all.

I had two particular fights of this kind that I won, which made me a champion-in-chief in two communities. These were not easy wins: one boy left me with red scratches along my neck. The second bit my lip, nearly removing the top part. I still have a scar from the wound on my upper lip. These victories elevated me in the boys' pecking order.

I was a persistent challenger. If a boy defeated me in a bare-knuckle fight, I challenged him to a stick fight. I figured that there was no way someone could defeat me with both weapons. Also, if a boy defeated me, it meant that every time we met we would fight again. I did not give up at all. These fights ended the day I was taken to the chief's house and given corporal punishment.

Our lives were not just about hunting and fighting for positions in the hierarchy of boys. We also spent summer seasons swimming in the river. We learned to swim without proper coaching from experienced swimmers. Their approach to teaching was to throw a novice into the deep end of the river, where the natural fight or flight response (a survival instinct) was expected to kick-in.

I nearly drowned because, while I was still in the learning phase, I accidentally jumped into a deep area and started sinking. My friends thought I was just messing around and laughed at me while I went down. Luckily, one of the older boys, named Shenke, realised I was in trouble. He jumped off a horse and leaped into the water to pull me out. It was disconcerting for my friends to realise that while they were having fun, I was at risk of death.

I'm not just sharing these stories to entertain you. I firmly believe that my upbringing had many instances where I was pushed to sink or swim, which has taught me to never panic in the face of adversity. The fights inflicted immediate pain on my body. And while fighting is not socially acceptable, I still took away something from the process: to stand up for myself, be willing to change strategy if the current one does not work (for example, changing from fist fighting to stick fighting when losing a battle), and to be persistent and give the fight another attempt if I lost the last one. Never give up! That was the key lesson there.

I further learnt that sometimes it is hard to latch on to something new when the teacher does not have a viable teaching method. We all know that throwing someone into the deep end (whether literally into a river, or into a life or work situation) and shouting "Swim!" does not transfer any skill from the teacher to the learner. Never mind the fact that it's fraught with danger: if the learner fails to swim, they could mess up the project or literally die. Sometimes this happens to the inexperienced at work, in business or even generally in life.

I learned that in the middle of a crisis, if I did not panic, I would be able to ask myself, "What can I do to resolve this situation?"

Finally, I learnt that even in situations where we think we have no resources, we actually do, although the resource may seem to have no value to anyone. My story about hunting rats is a good demonstration of that, where we collected seemingly useless information – where rats lived and moved – and placed traps for them. While I may not have had any use for the rats, my friends could sell them to practitioners of traditional medicine.

Another resource I found to be of tremendous value is the love and support of family and friends. For instance, I believe my mother's love helped build my confidence, which I needed to tackle new and challenging things. The love my mother gave me made me feel I was enough and I did not need to rely on strangers for affirmation. Confidence is not a tangible resource, but its results show when doing new tasks.

Her love also gave me the inner fortitude to socialise with some of the highest-ranking people in society without issues. Because I matter to her and the rest of my family and friends, the opinions of high-ranking people in society do not intimidate me.

This does not mean that a person is doomed to a lack of confidence if they lack family love and support. The key is to recognise that we matter as human beings, even if there is no one to reinforce that notion.

Just as my mother taught me that I am enough, I want to say to you through this book that you are enough. Accepting this will contribute strongly towards developing a conquering spirit.

Things for you to Think About:

1. What are the childhood activities you engaged in?
2. How did these activities shape you into the person you are today?
3. What lessons did you learn from the most memorable activities?
4. Do you still apply those lessons in your life?
5. Did you ever underestimate what your resources, which you deemed small, can accomplish?
6. Is there an instance in your life where a small amount of resources made a meaningful impact in your life?
7. What do you know that you can sell to raise some resources to achieve your goal?
8. In the past, when you were faced with a sink-or-swim situation, did you:
   a) Panic or give up and sink?
   b) Swim out of that situation through luck?
   c) Ask for help?
   d) Use what you know to get out of that situation?

Keep in mind that some solutions may not always be viable: asking for help only works if the people you ask are willing and able to provide it. There is no right answer to this question. This is about your life.

Chapter Six

Dream big

As I GREW OLDER, it became apparent to me that my community did not have resources for many leisure activities. So, I decided to start a soccer (football) club that would compete with other teams from other communities.

My aim was to enable the children in our community to spend time away from socially destructive activities by playing soccer. This was my first foray into launching a social impact programme. Although at that time I did not realise that this was leadership in the making, now when I look back, this is where I began to dream big for a better life, not just for me, but for other members of my community. I would also say this is when my leadership journey was realised at the tender age of twelve.

My duties as a football club coordinator included organising games with teams from other communities. It was hard, because we did not have a schedule for these games. Players from other villages simply showed up without giving us prior notice.

The club field was behind my home, so when a visiting team arrived for a meeting, I was the first to notice their presence. I would then go door-to-door to round up our players. Sometimes I found a player still tied up in household chores. I would then assist them so they could quickly finish on time for the game. There were times where I could not find all my players. The soccer games at times did not end with celebrations. Instead they ended with fights. Sometimes when a team was losing a game they would just take the money we were playing for and run away with it and we would go to our community and fetch sticks to fight with them. At times they were very strong and we would run away to one of the soccer player's houses and lock ourselves inside the house, looking through the windows until they had left our village. One would think we were playing for big money but we were only playing for 10 cents. I think the games were more about playing than money. We were only fighting for 10 cents but you would think we were fighting for R20 000 as fights at times ended with scars and lots of bleeding. I guess we were developing physical strength that would go on to help with life's endeavours.

Unfortunately, my mother was not as welcoming and supportive of this soccer idea as I had hoped. She viewed it as an ungodly activity. If she found me playing soccer on the field she gave me a hiding. To avoid conflict with her, while still participating in my beloved sport, I decided to play as a goalkeeper. This allowed me to see my mother approaching from a distance while she was coming home. I would then run home, clean myself up and try to look innocent. As the playing field was behind my house, it was easy for me to make the great run home before the car bringing her home stopped close to our house.

One day, my mother was home on the day of a game, and I couldn't join my team. It was painful to watch from home, especially when my teammates were losing.

I had big dreams for the youth of my community and longed to grow up in a socially constructive environment. I acknowledged that my mother's way of achieving this goal was different from mine. She thought religion was the answer but I believed sports like soccer (gaining the benefits of physical activity, working as a team and meeting boys from other communities without hierarchical fights) would be a key to our success.

I embarked on this venture knowing that the punishment from my mother would be severe. But I believed in this dream, and was willing to pay the price to see it to fruition.

***

My father also had big dreams for his family. He was very religious, a staunch evangelist and sought-after preacher. He wanted all his children to grow up in a dignified manner. Although he was not always physically present at home, he worked to make sure that the family had enough food to eat, a good education and school uniforms. This may not seem like a big dream in this day and age, where access to education for children is mandated by the law, but that was not the case in the past.

As a low-income family in the rural Eastern Cape and subsistence farmers, our food mostly came from the family fields and the family livestock. My mother sold sweets, clothes and chips as a source of extra income, which is why she asked me to assist by selling at school to increase her customer base and boost sales. My father's biggest dream was for all his children to gain an education. The fact that he fathered ten children who depended on his provision posed a major obstacle on the road that led to fulfilling this dream.

Big dreams were part of my father's "treasure chest" items, which I fortunately inherited from him. My siblings and I fulfilled his dream – we gained degrees, some postgraduate ones, and some are busy with PhDs. I am grateful that he witnessed his dream come true and attended some of our graduation ceremonies, in life sometimes what our parents wish for us they never live to witness.

It took hard work, overcoming struggles and a determination to never give up so that ultimately what was once a dream has become our reality. And it all started with one man's dream, who wouldn't dare let his circumstances dictate the scope and validity of those dreams.

I also learned to dream not just for myself and my family, but for the community at large. Although it is not possible to measure or demonstrate the impact those soccer games had on the boys in my community, I do know that we enjoyed them while they lasted, and those moments of pleasure and accomplishment accompanied me to adulthood. So, surely some of the boys also still carry with them fond memories of those ad hoc, local friendly matches.

In addition, I took note of this fact: dreaming big was not as a result of the resources I had at hand. I had no way to schedule games with teams from other communities but somehow I managed to have visiting teams playing with my team. It is indeed true that a willing heart can achieve the unimaginable.

Furthermore, it became very apparent to me that accomplishing dreams may take more fortitude than I thought it fair to ask of me.

Nevertheless, if there is truly a dream I wanted to bring to life, I had to work around and go against all challenges. In my case, my mother disapproved of my passion for soccer but I organised our village team anyway and suffered the consequences later.

In hindsight, I realise that people I thought opposed some of my goals did not really mean to do so. For example, I dreamed of a community youth soccer team. The bigger picture of this dream, which I may not have appreciated at the time, was that we as young boys in the community may engage in a socially constructive activity. If you think about it, my mother actually dreamed of the same reality, that we as a youth might engage in socially constructive activities. She just utilised a different vehicle to get us there. Her most trusted, effective and efficient vehicle of choice was radical Christianity. This is why she punished me when I engaged in an activity that she deemed sinful, never realising that we, mother and son, had in fact a very common goal.

In this context, developing a conquering spirit and dreaming big also means being able to see the bigger picture in any situation. This enables the dreamer to find unexpected allies to accomplish their dreams.

Finally, dreaming big is admirable but it is important to take steps towards making the dream a reality. It will take hard work, persistence, consistency and a willingness to deliver quality work.

You may or may not feel you have support from your loved ones. However, as you have read, we managed to create a functioning soccer team in our village against my mother's mighty opposition.

Support may also come from unexpected sources – the people in our village were not blind to the fact that I organised a soccer team for their sons. Yet, my mother never confronted me about that fact. The only confrontation arose if she caught me playing soccer. I would like to believe that the villagers knew never to discuss my soccer games with my mother and quietly supported me.

Things for you to think about:

1. What were your dreams when you were young? What did you fantasise about doing when you grew up?
2. What was your family's response to those dreams? How did their response make you feel?
3. What was the response of your teachers and fellow learners to those dreams? How did their response to your dreams make you feel?
4. What was the outcome from your childhood dreams?
    a) Did you give them up?
    b) Do you say to yourself, "If only I had pursued my dreams"?
5. How do you feel about your childhood dreams now?
6. Do you have new dreams or do you still harbour dreams from your childhood?
7. What do you plan to do about your dreams?
8. What is stopping you from pursuing your dreams?
9. Do you have a plan to pursue your dreams?
10. If you don't have a plan, can you make a list of things you need to do to accomplish your dreams?
11. If there are obstacles to your pursuing your dreams, do you have possible ways to deal with those challenges? They don't have to be guaranteed to work; just list some things that you know you can try.

Chapter Seven
Establish a culture of education

AN IMPORTANT ELEMENT of obtaining a conquering spirit includes willingness to learn from many sources and apply those lessons in our lives moving forward. My parents were key in ensuring that all their children received a better education. When we say our parents are heroes, that thinking is derived from what they have been able to achieve through us with little or nothing, but with a dream that their children can do better. When we look back and consider where we are through them we have no better words to express our gratitude but to honour them as our heroes.

One of the most important lessons I learned from my parents is that having a culture of learning in your family and in life is an important contributor to success. They established a family culture that when a child was ready for high school, they were to attend a school that had boarding school facilities. Keep in mind that learning is not just about attending school. The Oxford dictionary defines learning as "the acquisition of knowledge and skills through study, experience, or being taught."

However, my parents were subsistence farmers, and they knew that a formal education from school would improve our future prospects. That education would contribute to developing the conquering spirit we needed to face life's challenges. One of my foundation lessons is that there will always be obstacles whenever I seek to meet my objectives.

But if I keep my head down and just get on with the job at hand, learning new ways as I go along, success becomes inevitable.

One of the major challenges I faced during my primary school days was a heavy load of chores that had to be finished before I could even get into the classroom. My weekday routine was to wake up at 04:30, milk the cows and then lead the livestock to the grazing fields. If I was on cooking duty that day, I had to make our breakfast of pap and cabbage first thing in the morning, before milking the cows. The funny part about this is that there was not even a single day when we felt it was too much or felt overloaded. I am not sure why. Was it because there was no other way out or was it because we feared those who instructed us? Let me leave it as a topic for another day.

That was training for us to be physically and emotionally resilient and to dance in the storm when life's challenges hit us. The conquering spirit was instilled in those moments but we did not even know or feel it then. The last thing I did upon my return from leading the livestock to the fields was to clean the house. Only then could I leave for school, which was a 2km walk away.

If I was late for school, the teachers waited for us with a whip, as the school would not tolerate any late coming. I maintained this routine until I was 15 years old and moved from home to boarding school, where life was a totally different experience.

I'm explaining this routine because my family's culture of learning drove me to continue with my schooling despite all the other elements that made it difficult. It never even occurred to me that there was an option to quit school, because my family had made it clear that the only way I could improve my circumstances was through education.

As I mentioned earlier, learning sources also include being taught and learning from experience. So it was ingrained in me that I had to ensure that the family livestock came back home in the evenings. If they did not come back from the mountain, my mother would be waiting to whip me hard. She gave me corporal punishment until I was 13 years old.

I can still vividly remember the last day she whipped me. One of the sheep gave birth and left the lamb up the mountain and I did not notice, which was careless of me. That night the sheep made a lot of noise crying for its lamb. I woke up in the morning, went to school and when I came back from school my mother asked me about the lamb.

I said all the sheep and lambs were back. She accused me of lying because the sheep had made noise the whole night. After whipping me she sent me to one of the communities that we boys were rivals with to fetch something. At the entrance of that community I met one of their senior guys – the late Mhlangabezi Kiviet – who wanted to beat me. I was still suffering from the whipping pains and I knew at that moment that even if I tried to run, I would not make it, and that I still had to come back with what I was sent to fetch in this village. (It was called Umphambili, meaning "the front part". We were actually part of the same village. Our part was at the back so we were called Mva meaning "the behind".) I think he realised that I was helpless and just stuck his finger in my face and said, "You are silly!" and left me without beating me. For the first time and last time in my life I apologised to another boy.

* * *

Corporal punishment taught me that I can withstand a lot of pain and not break. One teacher tried to break me and make me cry. She was my Grade 2 teacher – the late Mrs Mafanya – and said she noticed that I did not cry when I was being punished. She vowed that day that she would hit me until I cried. She was strong and the other children were scared of her. But she hit me hard many times and I never cried.

When she stopped she said, "You have balls in your throat." Such physical pain endurance trained me to handle any other form, shape and size of pain. And my family's culture of education ensured that I did not run away from such intimidating situations, because my education was more important than the beatings that happened at school.

As I mentioned previously, my father valued education to such an extent that he also put his siblings through school. One of his sisters did so well in high school that she studied to become a teacher.

My parents appreciated the fact that our daily life at home was full of chores, and wanted their children to be in an environment where they were not distracted by chores so they could focus on their academics. So when I finished my junior level education, my parents enrolled me into Nyanga High School, a high school that offered a solid education programme with boarding school facilities. This boarding school was 220km from my home village.

I arrived later than the rest of the learners, as the school had a policy of prioritising learners who lived in close proximity to the school before reserving space for the students coming from afar. That means that my application to Nyanga was considered last and, as a result, I was accepted later.

By the time I could begin school, the classes that offered both Physical Science and Mathematics were full, which are subjects I needed for my proposed future career choice. Physical Science in Grade 10 was crucial for me as I wanted to study for a Mechanical Engineering degree.

I didn't give up on my dream despite this major setback, and the next year, in Grade 11, I changed classes to enrol in a class that had a subject grouping of my choice. This was hard to accomplish as I basically had no solid foundation to build on. Traditionally the school system operated on the principle that learners needed Grade 10 Physical Science to enrol for Grade 11 Physical Science. I'm not sure how I managed to accomplish the move. I call it a miracle. But I always go for what I want in life.

My friend summarised me very well at my wedding when he said, "Mdu never backs down on what he believes and wants in life. So if you are the person that Mdu wanted in his life, that is why you are here."

I knew that failing Grade 11 Physical Science was not an option for me even though I had a Grade 10 information gap. The school, which was a top academic school in the region, had a policy that if a learner failed any of the core subjects they were expelled from the boarding school. So to save our space at the boarding school, we had to work our socks off. The school also established a culture and environment of academics: classes paused at 14:00, and we went to lunch. Then at 15:00 we went back to class until 16:30. Afterwards, we rested for an hour and a half, and then went back to class again at 19:00 until 21:00, from Monday to Thursday. So there was a culture of studying hard at the school.

During my Grade 11 year, I had my work cut out academically and socially. I worked very hard in my academics, as I did not want to lose my place at the boarding school. I also did not want to return home to study at the local schools in Qumbu. My efforts paid off and I earned a place in the "Top 3 Overall Performers" in my class. I maintained a ranking position in my grades until our final year.

Nyanga High School still has a culture of excellence. The school's

2019 matric class achieved a 95.45% pass rate. The class also had 88 bachelor's passes, 38 diplomas and 21 higher certificates. They accomplished this despite the fact that the school is located in a rural village with limited infrastructure.

Another consequence of my late acceptance into Nyanga High School was that learners had already been assigned age – or rather grade – appropriate hostel rooms. I was placed into senior student dormitories, which I received as a blessing, as the allocated accommodation for first-year students was already full.

Many boarding schools had an initiation culture. Senior students would initiate junior students in abusive ways: some students would get beaten, have their sleeping mattress dipped in water, and so on. Fortunately I had protection because I stayed with the seniors, which saved me from new learners' initiation. I stayed with very strong guys, the likes of Ta-Mdu Ngcobo, Ta-Unza and Ta-Uhuru. None of the students wanted to mess around with them; they were the generals of our generation at the school.

There were days when the seniors were tempted to bully us but they said they were afraid that God would punish them for ill-treating a skinny and young person like me.

The school generally had very strict rules: boys were not allowed into girls' hostels and vice versa. If you were caught where you should not have been, you were expelled with immediate effect. Like every young person, I also succumbed to the challenge of peer pressure at high school. My friends smoked dagga and drank alcohol. I used to accompany them when they went for a smoke or a drink. But somehow, I was at least never even tempted into tasting smoking or drinking. I cannot explain why I had no desire for such tendencies. I guess it could have only been through the grace of the Lord. Also, my parents' church prayed for us. I remember every time we were about to go to school they would pray for us. I tell you, they prayed for us like they were praying for sinners that had already been caught red-handed.

I had always vowed to myself and stood by my decision to never smoke or drink. I suppose there was no amount of peer pressure that could get me to change my mind. I believe it was through the grace of the Lord that we were never expelled for these crazy adventures. We used to hang out until the early hours of the morning, and there were times when the police came and searched us for contraband while we were sitting in the hidden corners and yet they never found anything. One night we did something so very stupid we could have been arrested. My friends decided to go and smoke right by the police station entrance. I think all the dagga that night went to their heads, and wired up an idea to go and provoke the police. I showed a lack of judgement too and went with them. By the grace of the Lord the police did not come out that night. We would have been arrested for being in possession of dagga and smoking it. I thank God that in the midst of all those foolish acts, I remained myself.

***

Academically, I continued to work hard. When the teachers asked a question my hand was always up. In my class three of us always had our hands up – Lifikile Luke, Thembile Nobaza and myself. As a result, at times teachers decided not to ask for answers from us three, as we always participated and provided correct answers to their questions. The teachers said they wanted input from the other learners.

We had caring teachers who monitored our educational progress and came up with intervention methods when necessary. One scenario was in Grade 12 when my grades dropped so the English teacher, Teacher Ndamase, called me into the staffroom to find out what the problem was and if there was anything I was going through that was affecting my performance negatively.

THINGS FOR YOU TO THINK ABOUT:

1. Are there any systematic development challenges that were presented while growing up?
2. What were these systematic development challenges?
3. How did you overcome the challenges you faced when facing these systems?
4. What role do they play in your life today?
5. What are some of the things that your youth allowed you to do that were contrary to your culture of education?

6. What are the positive and negative lessons that you learned from the experience?
7. If you could go back, would you change your decisions then?
8. Are you still in the process of acquiring knowledge and skills in some areas? What do you want to do?
9. If you are content with your state of education, what are you doing with your knowledge and skills?

Chapter Eight

Recognise the pursuit of your dreams translates differently in real life

SOMETIMES WE SPEND SUCH a long time dreaming of accomplishing something that when we eventually accomplish it, it is disconcerting to realise that the dream translates differently in real life. A conquering spirit recognises this aspect of real life: it celebrates the achievement of a goal and takes action to remove anything that mars the final accomplishment.

As you will note, my dream to study Mechanical Engineering at Peninsula Technikon, now known as Cape Peninsula University of Technology after a merger with Cape Technikon, was borne many years before. I already knew it in Grade 10. My friends Pumezo, Phila and Thembela also wanted to pursue higher education. When our parents heard about our desire to travel to Cape Town to enrol in tertiary education, they were not impressed by our decision. The fact that their sons wanted to travel to study in another province, in the big city of Cape Town, was a big concern for them.

We had to negotiate with them to allow us to go. It was not easy to convince them to agree. We decided to negotiate with each of our parents as a team so we could strengthen our case. We had a door-to-door campaign. Despite their concerns, our parents agreed to our proposal.

One of the selling points that convinced my parents that the proposal could work for me is that I had family in Cape Town. But when we arrived in Cape Town and visited my father's brother in Khayelitsha, we were shocked by his living conditions. There were so many shacks! One of our friends was in such a state of shock that he even cried and said he wanted to go back to the Eastern Cape. The place was very disturbing. We had to counsel him and remind him we had travelled too far to give up now. We managed to convince him not to go home after a long meeting.

The life of sleeping in a shack in Cape Town was new to me. The shacks looked like the shacks in our villages that were used to keep equipment and to make fire. They were not appropriate for people to sleep in. It was quite an adjustment but we had to do it because circumstances forced it upon us.

When we planned our Cape Town study, we were very naïve in our approach. We were not aware of the logistics we had to negotiate at universities and colleges. When we arrived, we were required to pay a huge amount of money as fees. We thought academic registration covered everything only to find out we needed to have two registration fees. We travelled to Peninsula Technikon using a train from Khayelitsha, which was another learning moment. We had to understand the train schedules from Khayelisha, where to change trains and how to read the names of train stations as the train was travelling. But because of the heart and desire we had for academics, those challenges seemed like water under the bridge.

We arrived at Peninsula Technikon and were told that our applications could not be traced, and were advised to re-apply. Another challenge was communication: our English vocab was very limited and broken; we were, after all, just village boys. However, we pushed through the challenges and were at last accepted. My friend was accepted at the University of the Western Cape, which suited him fine because we would be neighbours, while I was at Peninsula Technikon. The two institutions were within walking distance of each other so we would see each other daily.

I was the only student among my friends who had a Nokia 5110, which I had won in a Coca-Cola competition. I became a receptionist by default for all my friends because our parents contacted us on my phone.

When I got accepted, my challenge was that my father had lost his job in 1998 while I was still in Grade 10 due to retrenchment. After I had completed matric, my parents had sat me down and explained that I would not be able to attend university due to financial problems. They proposed that I must wait for my elder brother to complete his studies first, then he would have to take me through school to complete my tertiary studies. I convinced my parents to allow me to come to Cape Town, with the aim of negotiating with my father's brother to assist me financially for my studies. I assured them that he would definitely assist me if they allowed me to travel to Cape Town to talk to him in person. That was another bit of naiveté on my part.

The problem was that I was accepted but I did not have money to register. I presented my case to my father's brother and he said he had nothing. I was therefore forced to call my parents to tell them that I had been accepted but did not have a registration fee. My parents had to sell a cow to cover my registration fee. The little income my family received was from my father's Toyota Van and Toyota Venture, transporting people from town to villages.

Upon completion of registration, I found out that both cars had been involved in an accident and were written off. The Venture's accident also cost people's lives, including the driver. As my father had used all his retrenchment pay off funds to buy the vehicles, and neither vehicle was insured, the accidents ended that endeavour as a source of income.

My additional dilemma was figuring out how I was to survive until month end since I did not have money for food or any financial support. At first I was excited that I was registered for the course of my dreams, until I realised that now that I had used all the money to pay the registration fee, I was destitute. I didn't even have money to contact my parents to tell them I had registered.

I learned about life logistics, stationery, technical equipment and instruments as an engineering student. I learned that sometimes the excitement that filled me for fulfilling my dream of studying mechanical engineering was marred by the challenges of life that I had never factored into my plans. My dream was bigger than my challenges, so no matter what challenge came my way it seemed small not because it was small but because my dream was just too big.

The reality of being in my first classes and being given a list of tools I needed for that class, such as a drawing board, drawing instruments, textbooks, all of which also needed money, was another kick in the teeth. Our lecturers told us that without those tools, we might as well deregister because we would fail the course. There was also the challenge of getting lost trying to find the classes and arriving late to class because of this.

I could have easily been demoralised and given up because owning textbooks seemed unachievable, considering that I didn't even have food to eat. However, the determination and hunger that I had for a better future was unstoppable. The conquering spirit that had been growing in me over the years helped me not to give up on my goal. My relationship-building skills and discipline also helped me to get through my challenges.

I borrowed textbooks from my friends at lunch time so I could do the required work as some of the textbooks were not available at the library or were very limited. I spent my lunch time on those books and asking questions from my peers. I had a study group made up of students who were also in a similar situation. So we worked together.

Anele was very good at technical drawing and Siyabonga just kept us company. That taught me that when you put your desire first in mind, the obstacles become a second priority. The hunger for success was so strong inside of me, I knew I could accomplish my goal of becoming a mechanical engineer. Throughout all the challenges, all I saw was the finish line. It is true that success is not about crossing the finish line, as one would not cross the finish line at all, if one could not overcome the periodic obstacles that pop up along the way.

My lack of food to eat was rather a serious dilemma if you think about it. Biologically speaking, a person cannot function at capacity if they are not well nourished. Additionally, hunger can be distracting for an individual, making it hard for them to concentrate. As my parents were not in a position to send me money to buy food, my friends shared their food with me. However, I was aware that they also had limited resources. So I tried not to eat at every meal. I ate only one or two meals per day with them, so that my needs did not overwhelm them.

I was not the only one in this situation. I knew of a guy who ate student leftovers at the student centre, but he did not last at the technikon because of his challenges. He did not come back after the first term of school holidays. So I knew it was not easy. But as for me, quitting was still not an option.

My friends were also crucial to my resilience. They constantly reminded me that we were in it together and would support each other through thick and thin. Some of them were my old and new friends and my study group kept me fed. They included Usanda Kewana, Pumezo Myataza, Siwiwe Tyokolo, Sivuyile Gwija, Anele, Siyabonga, Phila Ntantiso and Anda Bici.

At some stage my father decided to travel to Cape Town to look for work. No one would hire him for a physically demanding job because of his age. When the job hunt did not work out, he focused on preaching the gospel.

My father met the Nomaqumbe family in church and told them about me, and that I was studying at Peninsula Technikon, and struggling financially. The late Vuyani and his late wife Nontombeko Nomaqumbe pledged to assist me, even though they were not earning a lot of money, as they were just selling meat to survive. Originally it was their brother who was earmarked to assist me, but when Vuyani and Nontombeko met me they hijacked the appointment and I ended up not meeting their older brother Xolani Nomaqumbe. They loved me and took me in as their son. When June school holidays rolled in, I could not travel back home because I did not have money. A neighbour from our village who worked for the City of Cape Town and stayed in Langa township accommodated me. So, I went to stay at Langa flats, another foreign environment for me. It was tough but my dream pulled me through all these circumstances. My host in Langa shared a flat with a housemate and that housemate had two sons. Because I was new to the city and township life, they thought I would be someone for them to play around with. They made jokes about "the village boy". One day I got angry while my host was at work and got into a fight with one of the boys.

The flats were very small, so there was a very small passage between the beds that created a boxing ring for us. I overpowered him and beat him until he cried and apologised to me. From that day, they knew that I was no toy to play with.

I also had an incident once at varsity with my friend's roommate. I gave him a warning and he could tell I was not joking nor was I posing a threat from the tone of my voice. He never tried to provoke me again.

When December holidays came round and my parents did not have transport cash for me to travel back home to the Eastern Cape, I had to look for a job. I found it at a construction company in Durbanville where they were busy building apartments. At my arrival on site the workers looked at my frame and said I was too small to work construction. They appointed me to work as a storeman looking after the tools and building materials on site. My wage was R50 per day, and I worked for five days. It felt as though we worked from 06:00 to 18:00. The construction owner sometimes picked us up at 22:00 after the shift even though he was very punctual in picking us up in the morning.

Some days we left our homes at 04:00, but he would then take his time picking us up and would not apologise for picking us up late. Instead he shouted at us, asking why we were not working at the designated time for that day, while it was still very dark at night. He had no regard for us as human beings. At times we arrived home at midnight and were expected to be up at 04:00 to be ready for the transport.

We went to sleep tired and woke up tired. However, I worked very hard because my goal was to raise the cash to go home. I persevered until I managed to raise enough money to travel back home to the Eastern Cape. On a Friday I received my first wage of R250 for the five days of work. I took the first bus to the Eastern Cape.

***

One of the most important things I learned about poverty is the significant loss of time. It can take you three to four hours going around just trying to find someone to lend you R10 or work physically hard for the entire day for a wage of R50. That is why I consider being poor to be expensive time wise.

The reason I pushed so hard in life is I had a dream and my dream was simple. I wanted to break out of the poverty cycle, be married by age 30, have two children, and own our home and a car. The trigger for this dream was my parents. They gave birth to their last-born child when they were 45 years old and unemployed. I did not want to follow their late parenthood example. I wanted my children to have a different life from that. In a nutshell, the situation at home was the incorruptible seed for my desire and hunger for success.

I am very aware that our definition of success is different. To some, success is having something to eat, for some it is owning a house, for some it is driving a car and so forth. We all know our different personal versions of success. For my parents, success was defined as leaving their children with an education as their inheritance – something that could not be taken away from us. In my struggles at university, I saw that God provides. He might not give you what you think you want. However, He will give you what you need.

I also realised that God provides you with a community for every season in your life. I always had a community for every part of my journey. Even now, I have a community of people who surround me for every season. God knows best and He is faithful at all times. He is never late nor early. He is always on time and His grace is sufficient.

This did not mean I was free to sit on my hands, waiting for my community to share their resources with me. I eventually managed to land a job as a waiter at the Dros restaurant. This is where I practiced the art of serving and the importance of customer satisfaction. It was tough at times, working for long hours. The job required one to stand the whole day; my role did not allow for sitting down. By the time I went home my feet were breathing fire. But my willingness and skill to build good relationships made the job easier. We, the waiters, banded together and began to offer service as a team, rather than individually. Busy days at the restaurant could easily create a chaotic environment, and a solo waiter could end up giving poor service because they were not coping with the demands made on them. So, we decided to collaborate to offer excellent service. We looked after each other, and covered each other when too many demands were being made on an individual. This made everyone look great.

THINGS FOR YOU TO THINK ABOUT:

1. What was your dream career when you were in high school?
2. Did you enrol to study for your dream career?
3. Did your dream career turn out to be what you thought it would be?

4. Did you get employment in the career of your choice?
5. Did the reality of your dream career meet the expectations of your dream?
6. Are you still working in that dream career or have you changed the direction of your career?
7. What lessons did you learn from the pursuit of your career?
8. If you had a choice to go back, would you make the same choices you made while you still dreamed about this career?

Chapter Nine
Develop a strong spiritual core

I WAS BORN AND BRED IN a very strong, religious family. My late father was a tongue-speaking radical evangelist who was in demand as a preacher all over the country. Many churches flew him from the Eastern Cape to other provinces of South Africa to mediate in disputes and also to preach. I learned from my father about dealing with disputes by watching him in action.

I attribute the development of my spiritual core to my father, who actively worked to instil a strong spiritual foundation in me despite my resistance. Everyone in my family had to take part in religious practices. Activities included attending church, three days dry fasting, attending Sunday School Conferences, and night prayers. This took place between 15km to 20km away from our home. We were expected to walk the distance there and back and fulfill our home duties even on the early mornings that followed the night prayer.

We walked long distances for God but we were not aware that the Gospel of Jesus Christ was being instilled in us. We attended night prayers whether we wanted to or not. We were expected to be awake the whole night of the service, even when other kids fell asleep but not us Menze kids, our mother would be sure to wake us up unceremoniously.

We were forced to live for God while we were not even aware of God. I ended up enjoying church but could not attend most of the services because I had to take care of my father's livestock.

When I left home at 15 for boarding school, I did not identify myself as one of the born-again Christians. I only attended the monthly church services that everyone attended. At the time, the Gospel of Jesus Christ had not sunk into me. As they say, "You can lead a horse to water but you cannot make him drink."

As my parents always looked out for the best interests of their children, they suggested that I look for a church of their denomination at Engcobo, where I was studying. One Sunday I went to look for it accompanied by my friend, but we could not find it. I was relieved to have found an excuse not to regularly attend church.

So church became foreign to me until I went to varsity. At varsity my father felt it was time for me to commit to Christ. I refused. We had difficult dialogues about this and he could not win the battle because he allowed me to express my feelings on why church was not appealing and how come I could not believe in God.

I honestly and sincerely did not want anything to do with God. One of the major reasons was the fact that my family was holistically devoted to God and yet very, very poor. My question to my father was, "How on earth can there be a God that allowed us to sink in poverty?"

Each time we discussed God and the church, our discussion ended there. The truth was, we were very poor and my family was serving God; in order to have food on the table people made food donations to us.

Even though my argument seemed sound to me, it was a foolish stance because of my lack of knowledge and revelation. Now I know better because Psalm 14.1 says: "The fool says in his heart, There is no God. They are corrupt, their deeds are vile; there is no one who does good."

My father was still faithfully fasting and praying sometimes for 40 days but poverty was still core to our lives and, to complicate matters even more, he lost all his livestock to theft and death. So my argument to him sounded practical because I was presenting my case which was unfortunately also his own experience. However, he remained very strong in faith even during that time. He never stopped believing in God. He used to say that he wished that I had the same heart for God as I have for education. When I think about it now, I realise that it must have been very challenging for him for his son to oppose his life, because the Gospel of Christ was indeed his life.

We closed our discussions about my faith one day when he said, "I see this idea of God does not work for you. So do me a favour, and just pray." I promised him that I would do that.

My father was a very strong person. For some time, I did not understand how he lost this battle over my faith in God. But I understand now that it was not his battle but the Lord's battle. As much as my father was a strong person, he loved us dearly. When we had differences, at times he would allow us to do things our way after days, months and years of negotiations. He would eventually allow us to be who we wanted to be and he would say, "The reason why I allow you to do this is because I love you. That is all."

I believe that my strong spiritual core is a result of his prayers. I have never seen a person pray like my late father. That man prayed, spoke, breathed and slept prayer. That is the inheritance he left me. I can also pray.

So, my father believed in and trusted God even through hard times. He stood strong in his faith in God. One of our best qualities is that we take time to believe in something, but when we buy into it, it lives in us and we will not back down. We are very resilient. I have a strong belief system that I think influences my faith.

I started to attend church by myself while at university, even though I was partly influenced by my father's quest that I must at least pray even if I did not believe in God. I did not have a relationship with the Lord, but I had a very strong faith: I used to create timelines on things I needed to achieve and they would come to pass. For instance, my course required me to enrol for in-service training. I told myself that two weeks after my exams, I would have arranged it. It happened exactly that way. Anything that I needed, I just gave it a timeline and it came to pass. I have a gift of faith and I used it then even though I was far from the grace of the Lord.

I started going to church once a month in 2005 and I believed that the power I received at church on the first Sunday of the month was enough to carry me right through to the end of the month.

In 2005, while busy with my BTech in Mechanical Engineering, there was a subject that was so difficult it kept us awake at night. It was called Stress Analysis, done through a computer program. My study partner and I would sleep at the computer laboratory trying to solve problems. My varsity best friend, Lulamile Tshongweni, was doing Civil Engineering.

Having a girlfriend was not on my radar at that time. My plan was to only consider building a partnership with a woman I could end up marrying. One morning, on my way from the laboratory where we were working on the problematic subject, I met my friend Lula. He was walking with a woman called Dineo Lentotwane from Taung in the North West Province. When I saw her, all my good intentions to avoid girls flew away and I fell in love with her.

I approached her immediately and declared my interest, and told her I would like to build a relationship that might end in a partnership in the future. She was a very religious person, a Seventh Day Adventist. She obeyed her church's laws, which included not eating meat and not cooking on the Sabbath.

When I got to know her, I was attracted to her character. She was a very cool, quiet and collected person who was also beautiful, of course. I think she fell for me as time went by. She began inviting me to her church. I became a regular attendee. At the time I was a ballroom and Latin American dancer so I attended Friday evening services after my dance practice. However, deep in my heart I knew I would never convert and be a Seventh Adventist, because the type of Christian practice of my childhood was too ingrained in me to deviate from.

The Seventh Day Adventist church at Cape Technikon was also the place where the Word of God touched me in a different way. I'll never forget the message, which was from 1 Kings 3.9: "So give your servant a discerning heart to govern your people and to distinguish between right and wrong. For who is able to govern this great people of yours?"

I believe that somewhere somehow she fell for me, otherwise why else would she invite me to her church? But the big stumbling block to us getting together was our religious-related difference.

Love will make you do things that you have never imagined. I attended the Seventh Day Adventist church services on Saturdays because of love. I think Dineo eventually saw that I was just there for the love, not the religious conversion she had hoped for.

Though we never officially dated we did become friends. When she came back to varsity the following year, she was married. The worst part for me was that she married a guy who shared the same corridor with me at my student residence. He was also a staunch Seventh Day Adventist. I believe that they might be pastors by now. This journey taught me that in life no matter how hard you work for some things, if they were never meant for you, you will just not have them. But you get an opportunity to give it your best shot. Because I worked very hard attending church services and so on, I was sad that what I hoped for did not come through. It was a deep, cutting feeling because I did fall in love with her. But I had to accept the situation and move on. There is always a lesson for every season that we go through in life.

My journey to Christian conversion and development began in January 2007 with Prim. My brother's late wife, Nozuko Nomaqumbe, whom I called Prim, was a very talkative person. She could talk! Prim could talk until you fell asleep and when you woke up she was still talking. May her soul continue to rest in peace.

One day, she asked me to give her a ride to church. They had a Crusade scheduled for that evening. For safety reasons, she needed guaranteed transport to church and back home. I agreed to take her. It was my first time seeing a pastor preaching the way they did at that church. Pastor Bolumbe Chilogi was from Kenya and he was a guest speaker at the Burning Fire Evangelistic Movement, which was under the leadership of Bishop Fikile Dunga. Even though my father was a preacher and I used to attend church now and then, the experience was new enough to make me come back the following day on Sunday morning, 21 January 2007.

That morning I listened to Bishop Fikile Dunga of the Burning Fire Evangelistic Movement preach at the local radio station as he had a preaching slot there. His preaching convinced me to go to church and afterwards I asked my brother's wife to also iron my clothes so I could attend church with her. She was happy to do so because she was going to get another ride to church. She had been encouraging me to attend her church and now her wishes were being granted.

I received Jesus Christ as my Lord and Saviour that day when Bishop Fikile Dunga preached at the Burning Fire Evangelistic Movement, and my life was changed forever. The crazy part was that Prim was not convinced my conversion was for real.

"You were just following those that accepted Christ. I am giving you two weeks. I know you will stop after that," she said.

After two weeks, she gave me a month before I went back on my commitment to Christ. I am still in the house of the Lord 14 years later. It's amazing to me that she wanted me to accept Jesus Christ as the Lord and Saviour, but when I did she could not accept that my conversion was real. For me it is such an interesting thing that we recruit people for something, and after we have recruited them, we feel that they do not have what it takes. My question is, why did we try so hard to recruit them when we lack faith in their ability to commit to Christ?

It took me time to realise that when I became born again, I did not attend church as often as I should. The one first-Sunday-of-the-month church habit was ingrained in my system. One day, the then youth pastor, Pastor Xolile Ntsulumbana, suggested that I should accept Jesus Christ again, as I did not really convert to Him the first time. The youth pastor's evidence was that I was not attending church regularly as I was supposed to. However, I did not back down on my initial conversion, and am still serving the Lord today.

***

What kept me in the journey of salvation is prayer. It was the first thing I had known and I became acquainted with it again when I became a born-again Christian. That kept me grounded.

I also learned that having something to do in a group, like attending church, is a motivator to continue participating. Church also surrounded me with people who had a hunger for God, like Evangelist Mandisi Mtyhida. My father used to call him my pastor. Reading the Word together, and sharing the Word whenever we met as young men in Christ helped me build a foundation for my place in the house of the Lord.

I surrounded myself with people who had the same desire to grow in Christ. It was important to me to surround myself with people who desired what I desired, so that we could learn and grow with each other.

The church where I was serving was very big. There were more than 500 members at services on most occasions. So to be noticed someone must have something very special about them. One of the things the church leaders noticed about me was leadership. I have always had an old soul. They asked me to be the General Secretary of the Fathers' Ministry in 2009. They did not see in me a preacher but a leader. Especially as there were already many young and strong preachers at the church.

After three years of serving as a General Secretary of the Fathers' Ministry, they asked me to preach at the Friday evening prayer. I still remember every word I shared at that service. I was a bit nervous because I was going to lead a service in front of the pastors and people who were very mature in Christ. So it was a huge responsibility for me.

I turned to the book of Galatians 5.1: "It is for freedom that Christ has set us free. Stand firm, then, and do not let yourselves be burdened again by a yoke of slavery." I shared one verse straight to the point and kept the sermon simple and short.

I had also asked my friend Evangelist Mtyhida to conclude my sermon so that I could have a very strong finish. By nature I am a strategist. I had to be strategic to make sure that the preaching ended strong.

One of the key lessons I learned, and that I would like readers to take away from this chapter, is that to conquer your goals or achieve what you desire, you need to surround yourself with people who will teach you, share their knowledge with you and challenge you. When you are in the same space in terms of thinking and focus, you can inspire and challenge each other for the best results.

I also learned that developing a strong spiritual core is not an overnight event: it's a journey where you need someone to give guidance. Initial resistance is not the end of the journey before the end. There were also people of another faith on my journey who presented the case for their belief system. The lessons I learned from my father's belief system, which I thought I had rejected, to my surprise it was instead ingrained in me, helped me to continue on my spiritual journey.

The biggest lesson for me was that when you know you have found the foundation of your spiritual being – Jesus Christ in my case – you know. Some people may not believe it, and they may even have valid evidence for their position. But I learned that when Christ has changed the essence of who I am, and I am born again, it is done.

However, I also learned that accepting Jesus Christ as my Lord and Saviour is not the end but the beginning of my journey. The next step for me was to walk in Christ, growing as I was surrounded by my fellow believers, learning the word and sharing my lessons and theirs with them.

Another key lesson for me was that my spiritual life affected my physical life: the Bible served as the framework of how I approached life and how I responded to situations because God provided guidance through the Bible and the sermons by my church pastors, which were also based on the Bible. Accepting Christ as my Lord and Saviour also meant that I was never alone when facing challenges. He would always be with me.

Things for you to think about:

1. Are you from a religious background?
2. Are you a born-again Christian?
3. How did you become born again?
4. How was your journey on your first days of salvation?
5. How is it now? Have things changed compared to when you first became born again?
6. What would be different if you had to start your spiritual journey again?
7. How has your religious background shaped your life?
8. How did you develop a strong spiritual core? List the big highlights that you feel contributed to the development of your spiritual core.
9. What role do you believe having a strong spiritual core has in your life?
   a) How does it affect your day-to-day life?
   b) How does it affect your work and business environment and how do you manage that part of your life?
   c) How does it affect your interaction with your friends, family, colleagues and community?
   d) How does it affect your visions of your future, and what you do to accomplish those dreams?
10. How does having a strong spiritual core affect your daily life, work, family life and community?

Chapter Ten
Establish strong supportive relationships

ONE OF THE ELEMENTS of a conquering spirit is understanding that we can never accomplish our goals alone. We need to source support from all possible angles, family, friendships and communities. Such strong supportive relationships bring a variety of knowledge, skills and views that can help us succeed. Some people come into our lives by selective invitation in order to accomplish common goals, but support may also come from unexpected people and places. At times those we thought would offer us support may be the very ones who deny us for many reasons. Learning how to discern this at the beginning and be resilient enough to continue with the mission strengthens the conquering spirit.

I took a big step in my development on this issue when I was in Grade 11: I heard through the grapevine that there was once a family (the Mneno family) that had moved from my Qumbu village that was now established at Engcobo village, where Nyanga High School is located. I went to look for them and found them. That turned out to be a good development for me, because I became like a son to that family. They treated me as their youngest child. I love our relationship and always ensure that I stay in close contact with them. The father, Mr Solomon Mneno, the patriarch of the Mneno family, spoke as my father when I came back from initiation school. He bought me a Bible as his gift, which I still have today. He also spoke at my wedding.

I have a special ability to build relationships not only among my peers but also among families. While still in high school I visited a lot of communities where my relatives lived and built relationships. Those relationships are still going strong today.

In high school I had a best friend called Pumezo Myataza. We called him KO and he literally taught me most of the hobbies we enjoyed, from ballroom dancing to playing pool. We agreed in Grade 11 that we would gain our tertiary education together in Cape Town. He was going to enrol for an Accounting degree and you already know what I enrolled for Mechanical Engineering (Mech. Eng).

There was, however, a minor hiccup with my plan and the hiccup was my big brother who wanted me to rather consider studying Electrical Engineering. His inspiration came mostly because one of his friends happened to have done Electrical Engineering and was apparently financially successful. So he wanted me to follow suit and even study in Durban at Natal Technikon where his friend had studied. He wanted me to copy and paste the whole formula that led to his friend's success.

As you know, he failed to convince me to follow his plan, and I went on to study in Cape Town. As I've discussed, to study in Cape Town was a huge step for us, because we had never been there before and we were young. As we were staying at the boarding school, we needed permission to travel to town and to get permission one needed very good reasons. It was a logistical nightmare.

To avoid that mess, we decided to ask one of the girls who was staying in town to post our application forms. We gave her the forms and an application fee of R80 each. What we did not do was to ask her for proof of postage. We did not find out that she never posted our applications until our arrival at Peninsula Technikon. What a scam! I think she threw them in the rubbish bin and spent our R160 on herself. That taught us to never send people to carry out life-changing tasks on our behalf. Like I said, there may be people out there who will present themselves as supportive yet their actions will surprise you in a bad way.

Things for you to think about:

1. Who were your high school friends?
2. What attracted them to you and you to them?
3. What did you have in common beyond the fact that you shared a high school at the same time?
4. Are you still friends with them?
5. Who else is part of your support structure?
6. What brought you together?
7. What are the benefits that you bring each other through your relationship?
8. What do you wish you could offer the people in your support structure?
9. What are you doing to be able to add to your offering?

Chapter Eleven
Build a strong, healthy body and enjoy the benefits

THERE IS A LOT OF EXPERT literature about our need to build a strong and healthy body. Some people consider eating healthy foods and exercising a chore they know will benefit them, while others are not convinced that they have the ability and capacity to do it. Some people don't even have the interest, regardless of appreciating the theoretical benefits of it. However, an element of building a conquering spirit includes being physically healthy enough to meet the physical challenges of life. I needed to be physically strong and fit to be able to cope with the demands of being a server and working in construction, for example, and those jobs were crucial to my ability to meet my ultimate goals. Also, being physically strong meant that I could study for long hours without my body caving in on me.

Food and exercise can be a source of great enjoyment, even as we gain the benefits from them. In high school I tried hobbies that seemed unlikely to suit me. I tried boxing, but it was a tough sport. There were days of trial fights among us boxers, and those days took a toll on me. The trial punches were not really trials; they were fight punches. Though I never had an official boxing match, it was part of an adventurous exploration of sports to discover what I liked and what suited me.

One day I was walking to the student centre at university when I saw people dancing. Right then and there, my love for dance from high school was revived. I had learned to dance in Grade 12. There was a beauty pageant in town – Miss Spring – which was being used as a fundraising initiative by the organisers. My friend Pumezo was a dancer and part of the Engcobo Dance Club. The dance troupe was invited to provide entertainment at the pageant. I travelled with my friends to town to attend but found out when we arrived that while my friends were not expected to pay an entry fee as they were going to render entertainment, I was expected to shell out the cash.

I obviously didn't have the entrance fee, so I told the doormen that I was part of the dance club so that they would let me in. The new problem is that I was expected to dance. As life would have it, the dance partner of one of the dancers, Zandile Masangwana, did not show up. I volunteered to be Zandile's partner, making my claims to the doormen true. That created a newer problem: I did not know the dance styles or even the dance moves that the troupe were going to use. I had to learn them right then and there on the spot, which made life very difficult for Zandile, who had to carry my performance and cover for my missteps. It made her feel uncomfortable and unhappy. Life is a funny journey because later on in life I became a better dancer than Zandile and I achieved greater and more things in dance than her and yet she rejected me. Lesson here: never despise someone's small beginnings because they might turn out to be great.

We were supposed to provide entertainment at an event and I was in danger of causing her embarrassment on the dance floor. She decided not to dance with me as she had a reputation to protect.

The dance group at the student centre welcomed my enquiry and told me I could become part of them if I showed up for practice. They gave me the venue and practice time where I could join them. From then onwards, I began practicing with them and became a dancer.

Dance was an enjoyable pastime and I was very committed to the sport. We did ballroom dancing and Latin American dancing. Dance pushed my self-discipline to new levels, as these dance styles were very technical. Besides the technical moves in dance, the music was an engine that drove it. Ballroom and Latin American dancers have storytelling elements to them, because every move, the techniques and rhythm, have interpretations to them.

One of our dance coaches used to say, "You must dance such that a deaf person watching you must be able to understand the storyline – whether you love or fight each other." It also made serious demands on my body. Dancing regularly made me one of the fittest athletes around.

However, I struggled to find a partner, as my requirements were too steep. I wanted to dance with a very beautiful woman, in addition to her having a strong interest in the sport and great skill.

Eventually my wishes were fulfilled when Anela Majavu joined Pentech Dance Sport and she became my partner in 2002. I was not a natural dancer but I worked hard to improve my performance. Anela and I danced well together, until we reached a section called Novice. Novice falls under dance sections that are called open sections, where dancers wear the most beautiful and glamorous outfits. I swear you would think we were attending the Academy Awards in the United States. That is how beautiful the dancers' outfits were. I felt like everything about me changed when I was dressed up like that.

At my first novice competition, because of nerves, I forgot the choreography and just moved on the dance floor without a plan. However, I had a very calm partner, which was a great thing, because I had previously witnessed events where a dancer left their partner on the floor or cried the whole night because they forgot the choreography. She was also very understanding and did not freak out on the dance floor or afterwards.

Dance broke new ground for my development. I trained for dance under Kim Isaacs, one of the best dance teachers in the country, and later I trained with Kevin Juul, an excellent trainer who had great insight into the technical requirements of a dance and who was very calm. My dance career highlights included being a finalist in the Pre-Championship section in Durban at the World Trials Competition (a world trial is a competition used to select the top dance athletes to represent their country abroad).

One of the memorable moments at this competition was that they played the national anthem for the finalists. Walking in front of thousands of people on the stage at Durban International Convention Centre was one of my best moments in dance. We had danced hard and skilfully to make it into the finals in that competition, and the competition was fierce.

Dance is also a nerve-racking sport. During the competition, a dancer may be selected from the first round, but would still have to face the second and subsequent rounds. In the next round, the dancer's previous performance and selection from the prior round did not matter because they only served to make them eligible to be judged again. There was no room for complacency; we had to dance well all the time until the finals were completed.

One of my greatest highlights as a dancer at Peninsula Technikon is that I was nominated as the chairperson of Peninsula Technikon Dance Sport Club in 2002. During my tenure as chairperson, the club was acknowledged by the technikon as a Sport Club of the Year and the Most Improved Sport Club out of 23 sporting codes on campus.

I was also awarded with the Club Administrator of the Year award. That led to me being elected into the Student Sports Executive in 2003 as the deputy chairperson. From there, I went to serve on the South African Student Dance Sport Union as a coastal development officer, advocating the development of sport at coastal universities.

Dance also introduced me to new people and exposed me to different cultures, tribes, racial groups and communities. I made life-long friends through the sport. To mention one, I met Phemelo Mitchell in 2002 at the University of Fort Hare during the South African Student Sport DanceSport Union Competition. We formed a strong friendship that still lasts today. I also took my first aeroplane trip in 2003 when we went to take part in a dance competition in Johannesburg.

Dance was pivotal in transforming my university life for the better, as I met people who would go on to assist me through life issues beyond dancing. The central person in this development was Sydney Blignaut. When I joined dance, I met a new community that gave me a lot of support. It also took me away from the frustration of books and studying as a Mechanical Engineering student and gave me a platform to grow as a leader. It is where I relaxed and made great memories of my time as a student.

I left tertiary school a different person. I had earned my national diploma in Mechanical Engineering. Following that, I also completed my BTech in Mechanical Engineering and a BTech in Project Management at Cape Peninsula University of Technology.

THINGS FOR YOU TO THINK ABOUT:

1. Do you have hobbies that you do on a regular basis? What are those hobbies?
2. When did you start doing them and what impact did they have on your life?
3. According to you, is it important to practice your hobbies even when your life is fully packed with demands? Give your reasons.
4. What are the strategies you have tried to work around financial challenges that could, in the long-term, affect the state of your health?
5. Would you recommend your hobbies to someone else, and why/why not?

Chapter Twelve

Recognise that some detours will have meaningful impact

ON 28 DECEMBER 2008 I got married at the age of 25. I think it was too soon for me to marry spiritually, as I was still a new Christian, but the marriage itself aligned with my long-term goal to get married at an early age, and start my family early. That vision had nothing to do with Christianity. The reason I worked so hard in life was that I wanted to get married at an early age, start my family and grow while I am still young.

However, I learned through that experience that in Christianity it is better to have a level of spiritual maturity before getting married, so that when one is faced with marriage challenges as a young groom, one is able to withstand them. As a Christian I was expected to handle and manage my affairs in a Christian way and did not have the spiritual capacity to do so. I should have waited for at least three years to learn the basics of Christianity and gain strength in my faith before I ventured into marriage.

I learned that one of the reasons many Christian marriages fail is because people are expected to address and administer their affairs in a Christian way even when they are not mature enough to handle the challenges that marriage poses. They do not have the capacity to deal with their issues within a Christian context.

By September 2009, an issue in my first marriage took a toll on us. During the rainy season, we tried interventions like prayer, family mediation, pastoral care and therapy. Unfortunately, all those interventions did not save the marriage.

I have never begged a person in my life to be with me despite all that was happening like I did to my first wife because I loved her and had married her. I have also never prayed for a person as I did for my first wife and our marriage. And my family has never prayed for someone like that.

In terms of developing a conquering spirit, I learned in every battle, as a Christian, I was not alone. God provides a community for every season in your life; you just need to open your eyes wider to see. I had a great community that season that was with me through it all. They prayed with me, checked up on me, called me, texted me at times. There were times I was woken up with calls, just to make sure I was okay. It was one of the very challenging seasons in my life that needed that kind of support. That support sustained me throughout the journey of that season.

My father used to travel to Cape Town to be with me and support me while we were trying to address the situation. Those journeys strengthened our relationship. We began to know each other better and understand each other. It helped us build a better relationship in terms of understanding each other. We became close friends rather than just father and son.

The challenges of my marriage brought me closer to God. They also taught me, in a harsh way, that not everyone that was close to me and prayed with me was on my side. Some people presented themselves as supportive of me but they were there to collect information about the situation that could be used against me later. I knocked on the wrong doors, where I thought I could get help, only to find out later that they added to the problems. The Bible clearly warns us about such situations, and instructs us to trust none. Isaiah 2:22 states: "Don't put your trust in mere humans. They are as frail as breath. What good are they?"

That event affected my life: even today, I don't trust people easily. It takes a lot for me to trust a human. However, the positive part of that season is I grew in the knowledge of the Lord, as hard as it was. This is the season that shaped my spiritual life for the better. I grew and developed in the knowledge of the Lord. It brought me closer to God and revealed who I am to God and who God is to me. It was a season that revealed my calling as a pastor through dreams, visions, prophets. It became evident in 2011. Everywhere I went people with the word of knowledge and prophets approached me preaching the gospel that the Lord has called me and wants me in the field. But because I am a person that takes time to make a decision, I appreciated and thanked them for what they saw in me through the Lord, and did not respond to the calling when they said I shall. My true identity in Christ and my reason for salvation was revealed. The season also brought me closer to Pastor Vanya, who is my spiritual mentor now. It was the toughest season of my life. I could have been easily depressed and committed suicide. Remember, this was not just a marriage for me but a dream that I worked so hard for. So seeing my dream going through my hands could have left me doing anything. Some of the people who supported me through that journey are Bishop Fikile Dunga, Apostile Agnes Dunga and Mr Mzothando Mtikitiki, Mr Abner Mahlatsi, Pastor Zeyise, Oyama, Goodman Xabanisa and Evangelist Mandisi Mtyhida.

A conquering spirit also acknowledges good things that come out of a tough situation. Every little victory matters in propelling the fighter forward. In my case, although I lost the war for my marriage, I came out of that journey with some important love lessons. For example, no matter what you want from a person, you will not get it if the person does not have it or is not willing to give it to you. There is nothing you can do to make a person feel another way when they are not committed to change. You can love a person from the tips of your toes to the edge of your hair, but if their mind, heart and soul are not invested, that battle is lost. One of the strange or interesting things about love is, love chooses who to love. Maybe the saying that love is blind comes from that. Because at times people will not understand what you love about the other person and they will never understand it because love is also personal.

I learned to put everything in, to give all to my marriage. When I lost I knew I had done everything within my abilities and capabilities to save it. I emptied myself so that I would know I had done all I could have done. This applies to fighting for everything that we value.

I also learned to love and appreciate myself enough in that season to know who I was, so that I would not lose myself in the process.

Knowing myself meant I could lead myself, which is important because you need to be able to lead yourself in situations and circumstances. Also, I learnt that there is a point in life that one has to say that it is enough and accept a situation as it is and move on, and to understand that there is a point called enough in life and enough is enough. Accept and acknowledge that maybe, just maybe, my tries were not enough, could I have done things better or differently. Another lesson is that things do end even if you had great intentions about them.

I also realised that, after the divorce, I should have given myself the time to mourn, heal and recover. I think that is one of the things that we do not do as human beings. We do not give ourselves enough time to heal, mourn and recover. I should have just taken a sabbatical from everything. Maybe the life we live is so demanding it does not allow us to do that. But I believe it's something that should be done, because when divorce happens, we are hurt, the dreams that we believed in have just been shattered and we are drained by the whole process. We are still bleeding internally. We are wounded.

Despite all the challenges that came with that season, and as bad as it might have been at the time, the thing that left a permanent scar was being judged by society. I find our society interesting because when someone has divorced, they are labelled with uncomplimentary names. Even in the body of Christ, people look at you differently. When a person suffers sadly under such conditions (for example, due to gender-based violence in the home), the same society says, "Why did he/she not leave the marriage if it was not working?" And yet, when people leave, they are judged harshly for that too.

I think our society has not yet come up with the most viable way to deal with divorce and the people who have divorced. However, with time maybe there will be an answer. Or maybe not, because marriage is a delicate institution: a holy place that is honourable and holy to the Lord. It is a special institution that has been misinterpreted, mis-administered and at times misunderstood. The good thing is God with His infinite wisdom, love, care, kindness and knowledge catered for this in His Word so there is a clear Biblical view for those who are Christians such as myself.

Thankfully, that chapter of my life is over. What matters now is that I am blessed with a gorgeous wife, Dr Ayanda Mfokazi Menze; my wonderful children Nkitha Mbowane, Ezekiel Menze and Emmanuel Menze; and a gift of life.

THINGS FOR YOU TO THINK ABOUT:

1. Is there any decision that you have made in your life that did not turn out well?
2. How did you deal with the outcome of that decision?
3. How has your life evolved from the setback you suffered?
4. Has it changed your life in any way?
5. What lessons did you learn from that experience?
6. What would you do differently now?

Chapter Thirteen
The calling journey begins

WHILE I WAS DEALING WITH the battle to save my lost first marriage, I received the call of the Lord. It took me six years to respond to the call. The Lord called me in 2009 in dreams and visions. In 2011, the calling became more insistent: I was receiving prophecies from all walks of life saying that the Lord is asking me why I am not responding to my calling.

My response was that I knew that I was called but it was not yet time for me to respond. In hindsight, I can see I was destined to serve in the house of the Lord through His grace. My evidence is this, whenever I joined a home church, I was always commissioned to a leading role in the body of Christ. One recurrent office was being elected to serve as the deputy/right hand man to the senior pastor. This is the highest office second to the leading pastor, which comes with many challenges and opportunities; one's character is really tested.

I served in a position where there were spies looking for anything that I might possibly do wrong that could be used to flush me down the drain. I have been backstabbed, ill-treated, called names, lifted up, honoured, dethroned. I also burned myself in some instances. I began to understand the words from a football coach who once said, "Football can kill you, but church can finish you off." By the grace of the Lord, I have crocodile skin, and I always have a clear head in every season.

I think it's always helpful to have a clear head, with clear objectives as to why I am doing what I do. It also helps to have a clear understanding of who I am and what I stand for in what I do. However, I know when and where to draw the line and when it's time to pack my bags and leave, before losing myself in the process.

Importantly, I also never forget to honour those in authority and to love everyone. These are important boundaries, principles and values that, when they are being infringed upon, I am able to say, "No, this is not what I stand for," and move on before compromising my integrity.

My mentor, Mr Jannie Isaacs, normally says either you have integrity or you do not have it. There is no grey area. One thing I'm confident about is that I have never ill-treated the Servant of the Lord (the pastor of the church). When I felt that the relationship was broken and all avenues to repair it were exhausted, I packed my bags and left. Also I believe it is best to abide by the Word of God, 1 Chronicles 16.22: "Do not touch my anointed ones, and do not harm my prophets."

I experienced how my father was mistreated in the house of the Lord. Actually, his ill-treatment was one of the things that made me want to stay far away from a place labelled "The house of the Lord". I had also never wanted to be a pastor for the same reason. I still feel that, even after his death, there were instances that I felt were unfortunate. However, I will let the Lord be the Judge. I always advise people that if you know what is good for you, never fight with the pastor of the church. Leave the church if things are not working well between you and your pastor.

Mr Isaacs says, "You can win the war, but not the wall" meaning I could win the arguments on the biblical beliefs while serving but not the environment in the leadership and church. What kept me serving in church leadership was my consistent desire to do what is right, with a clear head. I am a very respectful person by nature, and my parents taught me discipline. I love the Lord and am passionate about Him. I am someone that spends a lot of time with the Lord. I always pray that He gives me inner peace every season. That is my pillar. As Philippians 4.7 says: "And the peace of God [that peace which reassures the heart, that peace] which transcends all understanding, [that peace which] stands guard over your hearts and your minds in Christ Jesus [is yours]." I also have a strong character, coupled with a resilient mental and psychological strength. Hence, I am able to conquer every season –

from troubles with people who seek to do me harm to the failure of my first marriage and more – through the grace of the Lord.

Things for you to think about:

1. Have you ever been in a leadership position, whether in church or something else?
2. What were your challenges?
3. Could you write down different instances where you used different strategies to deal with the challenges? What were the outcomes for you?
    a) Fighting until you declare a pyrrhic victory (a pyrrhic victory is where you win, but the price of the war was too high).
    b) Where you won fair and square.
    c) Where you lost but stuck around in that situation, unable to move on.
    d) Decided that there was nothing meaningful to gain in fighting this war and moving on.
4. What did you learn from these conflicts?
5. What would you do differently if you were faced with these challenges today?

Chapter Fourteen
Learn from your children

BECOMING A PARENT IN life teaches us important lessons in a big way and, in developing a conquering spirit, it is crucial to take these lessons to heart. Children are our future. They are one of the reasons we work so hard to develop and succeed at our goals. When we fail, we fail them; our success is their success. The things that we achieve on this earth should matter to people because they have mattered first to our children. So, we need to understand that we are fulfilling their survival needs, educating them, disciplining and leading them, and teaching them to be resilient and agile enough to adapt to the unexpected.

When I received the news that I was going to be a father, I felt that I was not ready because I was not in a good space as a person and still dealing with the aftermath of the loss of my first marriage. I was in such a challenging season. I was going through battles psychologically, spiritually and emotionally. I was not ready. My wife and I received the news together and I shed a tear not of joy but of sorrow.

It felt like the end of my life, as if the pending parenthood was a death sentence. In other words, I thought the time for me to depart from Earth had arrived and that the child that was coming was going to carry over what I should have done and be my replacement.

This was not because I didn't want children. My dream had always been to be blessed with two children. But the timing felt off, and I felt it was just not the right season. My belief is that we should be ready for the season of bringing children to earth and raising them. They need us financially, spiritually and psychologically, and if we are not ready, I fear that we would do more harm to them than good.

Parenthood changes everything. To raise children is a great thing to do, to be able to share yourself, share love and experience growth in the present. I have been graced by the Lord that my children literally grow before me, even before and as they were born. I have attended all their scans and I have received them, cut their umbilical cords, bathed, changed, piggybacked (ndibabeleke) them until they were ready to do things for themselves. That is how emotionally connected and involved with them I am. By the grace of the Lord they grow in my presence. The last born, Emmanuel, was received while my wife was working in Richards Bay. So she left him with me at the age of four months, and from then I slept with him, woke with him, changed him, fed him, and travelled with him to visit his mother at her place of work.

I call him my friend or personal assistant, and we relate as friends.

My sons are very comfortable with me as their father, but also as their friend. They climb me like a tree. One of my best moments with them is when I drop them off and pick them up from school and we use that time to talk. Ezekiel takes up 80% of our talking time, as he is the most talkative one between him and his eldest brother, Nkitha.

Also, I ask my kids to read the Word of God during family prayer meetings and monthly family check-up meetings. These are moments when we sit around the table and check up on each other: we discuss how they are doing, what their plans are, what they are busy with and so forth. Witnessing them expressing themselves and seeing them growing and hearing them saying that their dream is to be like me when they are older touches me in indescribable ways.

Being a role model to my children and hearing them say, "Dad, when we are old we would like to be like you" is a blessing.

But I draw the necessary boundaries as a parent. They are part of what I am doing, when I attend Waumbe sessions now (more is discussed about Waumbe later in this book) and then I take them along, especially the oldest one, Nkitha. Seeing him grow and gain confidence is an incredible experience.

Parenting is like running a marathon – it's a long journey. And raising children in our generation is complicated by the fact that they are exposed to social media, which can easily influence them. We have a huge competition with social media and society because they are very influential. My brother, Mzothando Mtikitiki, always says we need to teach them to unlearn some of the things. It is very difficult for them to unlearn things that they learn from social media and society. So we have to teach the children to unlearn their learning.

Our lives are moulded differently by the Word of God, circumstances, our upbringing, society and the family environment. I read once that we are 70% of our upbringing and the environment we were raised in. Whatever we learn outside of that impacts 30% of our personalities. I am not sure how true those statistics are. But that is a question for another day. Though there are a lot of sources available in the world today to learn how to raise children, the challenge is that reading about parenthood and experiencing it are two different things. All I can say is that raising children is an institution on its own that shapes our children for the future. We live in challenging times even in the body of Christ, which should be our baseline.

THINGS FOR YOU TO THINK ABOUT:

1. Were you ready to be a parent?
2. How is the parenthood journey going for you?
3. What is precious about being a parent in our generation?
4. What would you have done differently before you became a parent?

Mdu's parents, Amstrong and Nopasile Menze (credit: Senkie house photos)

Mdu in Grade 11, Nyanga High School, 1999

Mdu and Anita Sales, Fedansa KZN World Trials, 2007 (credit: Sydney)

Mdu and Liezel, dance photo, 2002 (credit: Virginia Dreyer)

Mdu and high school friend Pumezo Myataza, Peninsula Technikon (credit: Phineus Selebelebe)

Mdu's graduation, 2009 (credit: Gordon Harris)

Mdu's graduation, 2009 (credit: Gordon Harris)

Mdu, parents and siblings, 2012 (credit: Tamara)

Mdu and Ayanda's wedding, 2012 (credit: Tamara)

Mdu with mentor Mr Janie Isaacs, Waumbe Achievers Awards, 2014 (credit: Ayanda Menze)

Waumbe Youth Development Centre event, Fisantekraal, 2015 (credit: Kele Thebe)

Mdu running the Comrades Marathon, 2018 (credit: Jeline Action Photo)

Mdu and Pastors Ordination Service 2018 (credit: Mfundo)

Waumbe task team, Fisantekraal, 2018

Mdu, Ayanda and friends, Israel tour, 2019 (credit: Chloe Rizant)

Mdu with his grandmother (credit: Lundi Nikelo)

Mdu's Mom, Qumbu Mthozela Location 2021 (credit: Lundi Nikelo)

Mdu and friend Sva Tyokolo, Peninsula Technikon, 2002

Mdu's siblings, 2021 (credit: Lundi Nikelo)

Mdu and Ayanda with sons Nkitha, Ezekiel and Emmanuel, Cape Town Waterfront, 2021

2020 Junior Chamber International Top 10 South Africa Young Persons Awards, Durban

Chapter Fifteen

Building anything requires collective effort
(the Heart of True Worship International Church, a case study)

As you will discover in this chapter, planting a church requires a conquering spirit. The most important element at this stage was to have the understanding that planting this church was not about my goals and what I wanted to achieve. And at the centre of it all, this conquering spirit had to be based on God and his plans for all of us, which would be implemented in His own time.

So, as my story goes, after three years of serving at the Apostolic Faith Mission in Khayelitsha No.1 under Pastor Wisani, as his Vice, it was time for me to respond to the Lord's call. I went to see my now spiritual mentor Pastor Vanya and told him the time had come for me to respond to the Lord's call and to serve Him. I told him I needed prayers.

We therefore planned a prayer schedule for six months, starting from 7 May 2014 until September 2014. The new church planting was scheduled for October 2014. I took a six-month sabbatical but I was commissioned to work on a project in Botswana and the sabbatical was extended to ninth months.

Work at the Botswana site led us to February 2015. The prayer schedule was introduced, and we prayed three days a week, on Thursday mornings from 04:00 to 05:00, Saturdays from 05:00 to 06:00 and Sundays from 05:00 to 06:00 for nine months without fail. Even when I was in Botswana, I woke up at those times of prayer and prayed.

In the last week of January 2015, we developed and distributed flyers inviting people to join in the community prayer. I distributed those flyers with my wife and two of my sons, Nkitha and Ezekiel. The boys were so excited! Confidence levels were high because we knew that we prayed.

What we didn't know was that things were not going to go as easily as we anticipated. When we launched the church, I had Pastor Vanya, Pastor David Muller and Evangelist Mthyida as guest speakers. But people were not coming to our services. I remember one day when there was literally no one in the church seats, except for my own family members.

I went into the community and met a family of five who were sitting outside the yard. I begged them to come and join us and they did. The next session, I was afraid to invite a guest speaker who was used to ministering to more than 500 people, as I was afraid they would come to a zero-attendance service.

After the service, Pastor Muller called me aside and said, "It's not about the numbers, it's about the purpose." I was so relieved after that statement as it took the pressure off my shoulders.

The first Sunday service, my mother attended with my younger sister, our friend's brother Sabata Setoana and Dr Junia Moruri, who came to support us. On our way, while I was stressing about whether there would be people or not, my wife encouraged me by saying, "this is our first church service so if there is no one else in the hall, just preach to us. We are your first church, therefore, do not worry."

Building and establishing Heart of True Worship International Church from scratch was very hard: it took courage, perseverance, consistency and commitment. God was always faithful. He provided for us from the very first day. For our first Sunday service, God supplied three people from the community besides the family and friends who came to support us. He has been faithful since then.

The church has grown from three members to more than 130 people in five years. We achieved this through the grace of the Lord and very hard work. One of my takeaway lessons from this experience is that God provides for every season. God might not give you what you think you need, but He will supply you with what you need to achieve your goal for that particular season.

God provided us with the worship team that was led by Mr Sanele Dolo and his wife which were not the people that we thought would be part of our church plant. We had other people in mind who we thought would assist us, although we did not ask them. Because we were close we thought they would offer us assistance. It taught me that in life you can plan around people on your journey and they might just not deliver. I learned to be flexible and to adapt quickly. I also learned to never fix my plans around people because people could let you down at the last moment.

I learned not to expect too much from people. The Bible, in Psalm 118.8, admonishes us to "love them, but trust no one." It is better to trust in the Lord than to put confidence in man, and abiding by this verse helps. I also learned that no one owes me anything. Five years later, the vision of the Heart of True Worship International Church is to raise and release disciples of Christ who will worship God in truth and in spirit as per the book of John 4.23–24: "The time is coming and the time has come that those who worship the Lord shall worship God in truth and in spirit."

The church operates on several pillars. The first is the priesthood (the intercession pillar/priestly anointing) – this is a church that efficiently and effectively breathes, speaks, sleeps and eats prayer, which is our engine at Heart of True Worship International Church.

The second pillar is leadership (kingly anointing) – this is a church that not only believes in leadership and development, but practices it. We understand that knowing what is right means nothing until you do what is right.

The third pillar is apostolic anointing and deliverance; the conquering spirit here was demonstrated from scratch. Church planting is not child's play, especially because the place where Heart of True Worship International Church is planted is dry ground. The kind of territory where most of the churches have been started but then closed down and became abandoned because it is not easy to operate in the community.

The people in the community have a low capacity of desire for greater advances. They do not demonstrate feelings of being bothered by the extreme poor living conditions and poverty that marks their community. They show no interest in any of the developments that are happening or not happening within the community.

At times I asked myself, "What can be done for this community to get the people to have a desire for something beyond the experience of their daily life?"

To make headway, we had to be rooted in faith and mental strength. The first contributor to our success was consistency in our programmes, whether people were attending or not. This helped build people's confidence that we were there to stay. It also told them that if they wanted to participate, the venue, date and time would stay the same.

The second factor was our commitment. We were committed to doing what needed to be done to achieve our goals, even when we didn't see immediate results. The third contributor to our success was the courage to continue to put our time, resources and efforts towards our goals even when we seemed to be failing.

With God on our side, the church yielded the desired results after a lot of hard work and the right people for the job, who also desired to achieve our objectives. We were guided by 1 Timothy 2:1-3: "Pray for kings and all those in authority, that we may live peaceful and quiet lives in all godliness and holiness. For God wants all men to be saved and to come to a knowledge of the truth."

Discipline was also a crucial contributor to our success. There was great mutual respect among us working towards the common goal. Of course it was natural, and still is, for us to have disagreements. However, our common goal and desire was bigger than our differences.

My late father used to say that we will have differences along the way. We are not animals; we are human beings. However, what is key is the common goal that brought us all together.

There are people who were great contributors to the church's development. They were there from the onset and believed in me and supported me in prayer: my family, my spiritual parents, those who I look up to and those who offered services to us, such as training in leadership and development. They include Elder Gape Mogotsi, who served the purpose of the Lord with us, and Pastor David Muller, who supported us and offered words of encouragement in hard times and continues to visit the church as a guest speaker every now and then.

The success of the church was due to collective efforts from the church leadership. My underlying philosophy was of development, love, prayer and being a student at all times. I learned every day from the church members and leaders. It is not easy to lead. It comes with a lot of responsibilities.

Leadership is not for the fainthearted. By nature I take time to talk. I give time to situations until I find the wisdom to solve a problem and the best way to address it.

Also, one of the gifts that the Lord has graced me with is a way of addressing things in a calm, polite and loving manner. I have developed and raised leaders at the Heart of True Worship International Church who I am confident will be able to lead themselves first and then lead others well wherever they go.

Leadership starts with leading yourself before leading others, and also succession. I have someone who can lead at Heart of True Worship whom I have developed over the years and shares my office in many ways. He is very calm and quiet with a golden heart and a heart for God and for serving others. My Timothy is there and ready.

There were challenging seasons. We lost people on the journey that I thought we should not have lost. However, my philosophy is simple: when you come to Heart of True Worship International Church, we must develop you, give you opportunities, love you, teach you and serve you. Therefore, when you leave I owe you nothing and you owe me nothing. That is my motto.

There are times when people who leave say things about you. The important thing as an individual is to make sure that if they say bad things about you, what they say is not true. Time will tell, and the truth does not need to be defended; it defends itself when the time is right. But some people lie. I believe that what has been said about me is less than what is still going to be said about me. So I have had to develop a thick skin.

I had to discipline people who were very close to me when I felt they stepped over the lines drawn by the values of our church. The discipline was not because they were bad people; they just did what was not warranted. After carefully observing the situation, I called them and confirmed the principles of the Lord that we abide by and explained how and why what they did was not in line with God's word. However, I also made it clear that I would be there to support them and give them all the necessary support to overcome any challenges.

I believe that in the journey of salvation some of us will be stronger than others in some seasons, and carry those who are weak and facing challenges. Those who were strong before might face temptations along the way and be carried by those who were weak. We should therefore never be so short-sighted on the journey of salvation to believe that we will never need the strength of others, for the journey is too long. 1 Kings 19.7 says: "Then the angel of the Lord came again a second time and touched him and said, 'Get up and eat, for the journey is too long for you [without adequate sustenance]'."

Serving a church and having a family to lead, I need the grace of the Lord to try my level best to be a husband to my wife, father to my children and a child to my family.

What I would have done differently at the Heart of True Worship International Church is to patiently wait for people to mature spiritually before placing them in church leadership. Church leadership requires a certain level of spiritual maturity. Some of the people have left the church because they were put in leadership roles before they were ready. I did that because, I am a human developer by nature. In retrospect, I should have applied my mind to strict criteria before appointing them. I have learned the hard way; I've paid the school fees and, no matter how tempting, I will not put any person in the church leadership that has not reached a certain level of maturity, as guided by 1st Timothy 5:22: "Do not hurry to lay hands on anyone [ordaining and approving someone for ministry or an office in the church, or in reinstating expelled offenders], and thereby share in the sins of others; keep yourself free from sin."

The other thing I wish I had done differently is to maintain a high level of privacy, because at times people do not understand where boundaries are, so when you open up they might perceive that as an invitation to step over the boundary. By nature I am a soft person, leading in this generation with a soft character. It has its challenges especially when dealing with people who do not respect other people's boundaries. I have learned that sometimes I should just draw the line quicker and earlier rather than slower or later, particularly when one has stepped too much on my toes. But I still love and honour human beings despite our shortcomings. We lead in very sensitive and challenging times and we therefore need to be extra careful about how we communicate our message to others to avoid being misquoted and having things taken out of context.

THINGS FOR YOU TO THINK ABOUT:

1. Have you discovered your purpose in life?
2. How did you discover that purpose?
3. What were the challenges you faced when embarking on your purpose?
4. How did you overcome the challenges you faced when you ventured into pursuing your purpose?
5. Are you still serving your purpose?
6. If you are not pursuing your purpose in life, if you were given a rewind in life, would you make different choices? Why?

Chapter Sixteen
Build a strong capacity for leadership

As I've explained earlier in this book, my perception of what strong leadership is comes from my father. He was a strong leader in our family, the church and community. While he had a strong character, he was not arrogant. He was a great listener and influencer who never gave up on his beliefs. One of the things that he preached at family meetings was unity and collaborative work. He always encouraged his children to work together on any family projects because he believed unity would be most effective. After all, together we can do more. I internalised that lesson, as a result I easily joined study groups while at university and fostered teamwork among my fellow waiters at the Dros. My father also believed that prayer has a strong influence on leadership. He was influenced by prayer, and he was a man of prayer. He breathed, spoke and slept in prayer. He literally prayed for everything. Just to give you an idea, my younger brother used to fall all the time as a baby and my father said, "Come, I need to pray for you so that you can stop falling all the time." And he stopped falling all the time. The prayer worked! Prayer helps you to live a peaceful life, even when you go through challenging seasons or leading through difficult times you will be calm and patient because of prayer. Prayer helps you to lead with a clear head. You have a clear perspective because you are guided by the Lord.

My father led the home front with love, for what will profit a man who leads nations while leaving his own family behind. Above all, he loved us as his children. He constantly checked on us as his children, even his daughters- and sons-in-law. As a man who came from the generation of old, with strong cultural beliefs, he was surprisingly relevant even for this generation. He would call his daughters-in-law to check upon them and go as far as giving them names. For instance, my brother's wife's name was given by my father. Traditionally the name of a daughter-in-law comes from elderly mothers of the family but my father said he would give them names.

Another example is that he was part of lobola negotiations even though by tradition he should not have been part of the delegation for negotiating for us as his sons. Instead, he was supposed to send his family elders. He would say that he wanted to be part of his children's life in every way he could. When I had issues in Cape Town he would travel to come and be with me just to make sure he was there to support me physically. He would say, "This issue needs me to be close to you."

When we would travel home to visit from Cape Town, he would not sleep. Now and then he would give us a call to check up on us and see how far we were.

We would receive a call around 02:00 while driving and he would say, "I am just checking up on you. How far are you? Is everything okay?" He would conclude by saying, "I am praying for you." When we approached home, he would be standing at the gate ready to open it for us.

He would greet us and say, "Come in. Let us thank God for carrying you through." After that he would ask what we had brought for him. He loved himself, he would say, "You want to say that you passed all these towns without thinking of me?" His favourite drink was Schweppes Dry Lemon so we always made it a point to carry it for him. When we gave it to him, he would say to my mother, "You see, Nopasile, my children know me very well. They brought me what I really needed. You see, today I will sleep very well."

My parents' characters complemented each other. My mother's contribution is a soft, tender heart. She is not only a mother to her own biological children. There were always other children living with us when we were growing up. One wonders if ten children were not enough for her! Even now when I go home, I find new faces. It can only be love and a huge heart that would enable someone to raise so many children under the socioeconomic conditions she lives in. She also has to face the psychological demands of parenting, because having children from different backgrounds requires one to have a strong psychology. She is not outspoken, and takes long to speak up about things that bother her. My father, on the other hand, was more prone to taking the bull by the horns. He would not go to bed without addressing an issue that was bothering him. He would drive far distances at night to address an issue. If an issue was being addressed but common ground had not been reached, he would insist that they should not close the meeting with grace because it would create an impression that they have reached consensus though they have not done so. He even discouraged shaking hands until the matter has been resolved. This brought a sense of urgency to those involved to make sure that the matter in conflict was resolved soon.

They were not perfect parents. After all, they were human. But they were great parents and accomplished a difficult task in raising ten children with six university graduates, some with postgraduate degrees and some currently studying for their PhDs. This was despite the fact that they had never stepped foot at school. As I emphasised at the start of this book, my parents' goal was to leave their children with an inheritance that no one could take away from them: education. My mother always said these words when she encouraged us. My father instilled in us a strong sense of fulfilling mandates: setting goals and achieving them, and not giving up. When he put his mind to something, he did not back down. He had a way of saying things in his strong character. He was a very wise man. If he decided in the morning that night we needed to go and pray at the mountain, even though we had events during the day and got back home at 22:00, then we would go. When we'd get home tired from the event, you would think he would say "Let us rest, we are tired!"

"Not a chance," he would rather say. "Make yourself warm. We are going to the mountain for prayer. It is not right to promise something and not do it. I promised God that I would go and pray at this time, so we have to go."

We would go to the mountain at twelve midnight and at times it would be freezing. We would pray until 03:00.

When we were praying and we were tired, he would say, "Guys, you have to be intentional, be strong. You cannot pray this way."

Even in his last days on earth, his last Thursday on earth before he passed on Saturday morning, we went to pray at the mountain here in Cape Town. We were at the mountain until 03:00 in the morning. It was so cold that we hid ourselves in big rocks while we prayed and got back home around 04:00.

The inheritance he left me with is prayer: the key that unlocks every door and sphere when done appropriately and effectively. Prayer was everything to him.

Even his last words to me were, "You must never stop praying. We will continue praying so that whatever challenge you are facing as a church leader you will overcome."

Even when he arrived at the hospital after the accident, as he was taken by community members to the hospital at his arrival, they told me, he said, "Let us pray."

The very last words he said were that he is tired, can they please turn him around as he was laying on one side. He wanted to be turned over but the hospital staff refused. Minutes after that, he became restless and left to be with the Lord just after midnight. They estimate it was around four minutes past twelve on 1 April 2017. May his soul continue to rest in peace. What a Soldier of Faith, the Radical evangelist, Amstrong Kebetu Menze.

***

My leadership traits are from him. When I am not happy about something, my emphasis is always to objectively look at the facts.

I believe that a leader must be a strategic visionary: they must have the ability to see things in the future and capture them with a bird's eye view. I am currently driving a 50-year vision that I will hopefully conclude in 2065. I will be 80 years old by then. The vision is to plant 12 churches and Waumbe Youth Centres across the globe. The plan is to plant a church and a centre every five years, work on it for five years, and identify a leader to take over so I can then provide oversight within those five years. As of now, here in South Africa I have done the first five years of church planting and Waumbe Youth Development establishment. Both these organisations have leaders to take care of them. My next step is Malawi. I will be working in Malawi for the next five years to plant the Heart of True Worship International Church and establish a Waumbe centre. After I have concluded the 50-year vision, my job then would be travelling and visiting the churches and centres for review and impartation.

Finally, my capacity for leadership was strengthened by my ability to have healthy relationships across all ages and classes, as I have elaborated on in previous chapters. I have the ability to build friendships with many people, from juniors to seniors, whether they live in Fisantekraal squatter camp, Nyanga Township shacks, Plattekloof, Constantia or Bishops Court. I treat people as human beings irrespective of their race, ethnicity and socioeconomic status. One of my gifts is building relationships, for the advancement of a development agenda. By the grace of the Lord I happened to be connected and surrounded by great individuals with insight, wisdom and experience. The likes of Abner Mahlatsi, Louis-Delien Pienaar, Delphino Machikicho, Karen Zaaiman, my wife, and my mentor, Jannie Isaacs. These people get the best out of me. You have to apply your mind when you are about to engage with them. Once Louis pulls her hair, you know you are about to receive a question that requires great thinking. When Mr Abner says, "Wait, wait, I do not understand," this is a fasten-your-seatbelt time because a tough question is about to follow. My mentor will say, "Mdu, what I am going to say, you might not like it, but I will tell you anyway: you must know the hard truth is about to come. Hold your chair tight." These are the people who mould me every day: people with integrity, values, principles, and who are loving and caring; they serve from the heart. They make me a better person.

They do not take a wishy-washy, half cooked approach. Either it is or it is not, no grey areas; it's either go big or go home. At times, they question you as if they are interrogating you.

"How did you come to that particular decision?" They will say, "Go and think about it but do not give an answer now." There are times when I am on the way to meet them that I pray. That is how tough they can be, not in a bad way but just because they want the best from you. When the going gets tough, my mentor will say that "great pilots are made in bad weather". There are times I leave meetings with my mentor feeling deurmekaar, which requires me to sleep before I can engage again in any matters of life because of all his questions. But he always gives a cushion, a safety net. That is the sign of a good leader.

***

I am not scared of challenges. When I approached my wife asking for her hand in marriage, one of the things I said to her was that I had been looking for someone who would challenge me, get the best out of me and keep me on my toes. She does that exceptionally well. She is very intelligent, so when you are going to engage with her, you need to have a clear head and be attentive when listening. My source of strength comes from the Lord and I am running my own race with clear goals and executing plans that are intentional.

We can have many mentors in life. I look up to my mentor, Mr Jannie Isaacs: he is such a giver. When he gives you something he goes all out. I also look up to Mr Patrice Motsepe, although I have never seen or met him in person. I have, however, met his wife. It was at Cape Town Fashion Week. She is a very warm and kind person. What inspires me about Motsepe is his giving heart and generosity. I think he is very generous with a humble character from a distance. I hope to meet him in person one day. Spiritually, I look up to Bishop Katshunga Tshalo. He is a man with a vision. I have had the privilege to be in his presence, be taught by him and to be in the same space with him. He is humble with a clear, high head.

THINGS FOR YOU TO THINK ABOUT:

1. Who has had the biggest influence in your life?
2. What influence do your parents have in your life?
3. Where do you get your source of strength?
4. Who is your role model?

Chapter Seventeen

Find a mentor who can help you grow

IT SHOULD BE CLEAR BY now that I believe strongly in mentorship. My apparent softness has at times caused me to leave some issues unaddressed, which causes problems now and then. But the good thing about taking time to address conflict is that it allows me to fully observe a situation and apply my mind before I act. I can observe and contemplate a situation for years without addressing it, so that by the time I address it, I am confident of my position and the course I want to follow moving forward. I believe that timing is everything; whether this is the right thing or not allow time to judge. My mentors have helped me think things through, helping me to define the values that would influence my actions and response to a challenge, as well as charting a course of action.

Let me tell you a bit more about my mentor, Mr Jannie Isaacs, who maintains that things must be done right. He always says to me, "Mdu, there is a difference between doing something good and doing something right." If you give Mr Isaacs a document to review for you, you would swear it is not the same document by the time you are done working on it with him. His work ethic demands that you too deliver quality work.

I was introduced to him by the former Peninsula Technikon Vice Chancellor Professor Brian Figaji. When the Waumbe vision was laid in my heart in 2013, I went to Professor Figaji to pitch it to him.

He said to me "I think the best person to speak to about this vision is Mr Isaacs." When I contacted Mr Isaacs, he was in Norway for a project and he responded that we would meet when he returned. I had never seen him before this engagement, and had no clue what he looked like. He came back and we met. I presented my vision and he said to me, "Mdu, I must say, you must have very deep pockets. You need to know that you are going to compete with technical colleges on this project."

My vision, then, was to build technical skill centres in communities, to equip young people to be able to get employment opportunities. It was triggered by seeing young people sitting on the street corners doing nothing, the school dropouts from pre-primary up to varsity and college who are sitting at home doing nothing. They are ticking time bombs waiting to happen: those people sitting on the corner or at home have nothing to lose. The most dangerous types of people on earth are those who do not fear anyone and have nothing to lose. Someone who will do anything in life without applying their mind. My vision was to address this issue. After intense consultations and vigorous meetings, Waumbe Vision was refined and evolved to what it is today: a youth development centre to equip young people to make informed decisions about their lives, careers and so forth. A youth with hope and purpose. "Waumbe" is a Swahili word meaning "empower them". It came from my associate and co-founder Delphino Machikicho. I call him "The Workhorse". He is such a hard worker he always gets things done. He can work right through the night. To develop this vision took six months. At times I would come back from a meeting not even knowing what I knew because of questions levelled at me. If I was drinking after those meetings I would have taken the strongest of the strongest drinks. That is how hectic the meetings were.

Mr Jannie Isaacs has been instrumental in Waumbe formulation from the beginning, from registering the company, to setting up the board of directors and now leading the board as the chairperson. He is someone I am free to talk to about anything without fear of being judged and to be given honest and sincere guidance.

At times I could see that Mr Jannie Isaacs sensed that it was not easy. He would say, "It's okay, Mdu," and give me a strong handshake, saying, "Take care." He is a true family man. His first question in any meeting or phone call is, "How is the family doing?" He goes so far as asking how my mother and my mother-in-law are doing! He always says, "Keep your wife close and your mother-in-law even closer."

Now I do the same thing when I meet people and when I call them. "Mdu," he says, "life is about relationships." If we are having a meeting and something comes up that is related to the family he tells me to sort that out first: "We can always engage later, make sure that everything is sorted and that your family is safe. "He is not just a mentor to me but a father, as I no longer have a biological father. His love eases my thirst for a biological father. It's funny because I am a Xhosa person and now I have a coloured father! That is how life is. It's a journey.

He is a clinical person who works very hard; in his house he is a handyman and very family-oriented and he loves his children. One day my associate Delphino and I were talking about something that Mr Jannie did for his children and Delphino jokingly said, "He must meet my father. They have to have coffee so that my father can follow suit!" He is also a man of integrity. He always says to me, "Mdu, it's either you have integrity or you do not. There is no 'in-between integrity'."

He taught me the importance of quality work, including how one should communicate. When he gives me feedback on my work, he says, "Mdu, I will be critically honest with this work. Then you must know that, there are really shortcomings in your work." But he will guide me, not just throw me under the bus or leave you alone.

THINGS FOR YOU TO THINK ABOUT:

1. Do you have a mentor in your life?
2. What do you think is the role of a mentor?
3. How has your mentor shaped your life?
4. What are the characteristics of your mentor?
5. What do they add to your life journey?

Chapter Eighteen

Be brave and take a chance: Travel to expand your horizons

FOR MANY PEOPLE FROM poor backgrounds, landing a well-paying job is a dream come true.

However, that well-paying job comes with its own set of problems, which can easily tarnish the shininess of the dream. One of the issues is that you are not in charge of your work life; your employer is in charge.

I developed an interest in entrepreneurship in my final year of university, which was influenced by my father. He said, "If you are going to work for someone your progress in life will depend on that person. You can only develop and prosper as that person wishes to make you prosper. He is going to determine your development and income, when to hire and fire you. He will manage you." He was inspired by his friend Xolani Nomaqumbe, who was an entrepreneur. That planted an idea for me to pursue a BTech in project management with the hope that I would learn about business. I also registered a business and bought shares with Phuthuma Nathi in 2007. My father strongly supported this development.

He said, "You know, Mdu, this thing of working for someone else, you will be a slave forever. There is a young man in our area who started a construction company and he is doing very well. You should also start your own business."

***

On 13 February 2006, I started working as a junior mechanical design draftsman. I registered my first business in 2007, focusing on project management, but decided to hold off launching operations until I had the experience and financial stability to help the business succeed.

When I started working as a draftsman, the company director asked me if I had a driver's licence. When I said no, he said, "You are not fully qualified until you have a driver's licence." My work demanded travelling to different sites as a draftsperson to take measurements. Not having a driver's licence was a challenge as someone had to drive me to site, which meant that person left work, which was a loss to the company. I would lose time on site as well and so would the person who accompanied me, who would just drop me off. At times I would finish what needed to be checked on site while the person was rushing to work and when I would call the person to come back and pick me up, I would often have to wait for hours. In most cases, sites were not accessible by public transport. That forced me to learn to drive and acquiring my driver's licence changed my life.

***

In 2008, I felt that my experience and qualifications brought great value to my employer. However, I was unhappy with the remuneration package. I felt they were paying me based on their perceived value of someone living in Khayelitsha travelling by train to work. I therefore engaged the HR manager. We fought very hard at those meetings. I am a calm person but just wait until my calmness is challenged to the core. We fought a good fight. At times he would call a Black director and say, "Go and talk to this young man. You guys should understand each other better as Black people." I think something bad entered his head because he thought the Black director and I would understand each other since we are of the same race. After those harsh consultative meetings, there were good outcomes. That year I received a 39.5% increase. And I mean 39.5% after several meetings of battles. On that high note, that same year, De Beers Marine recruited me as a mechanical design research engineer. Here, I worked as a Research and Development Engineer on a new mining tool that the company was exploring at the time. That is where I met Mr Abner Mahlatsi and Mzothando Mtikitiki, who is more than a brother to me. Maybe the reason for joining De Beers Marine was just to meet them for they have contributed a lot in my life growth and development. Unfortunately, the 2008 financial crisis affected the continuation of the project and, ultimately, I was retrenched in March 2009, one of the toughest seasons of my life. But the Lord was gracious. I received employment while I was still serving the retrenchment notice period. I joined Paterson & Cooke as a mechanical design draftsperson from April 2009 until March 2011.

***

I began a new journey as a mechanical project engineer at ADP Projects in April 2011. This turned out to be a significant year in my life. My time at ADP helped me gain a lot of experience working on projects across the African continent. My first project was based in Lesotho, which required me to travel there. We arrived in July, which was in winter. It was my first time crossing the borders of the country, and experiencing such extreme cold temperatures. It was freezing, especially in the morning and in the afternoon. When we walked into the plant in the morning everything was literally frozen. The water would not come out of the water lines because they were frozen. The people were very warm though; they would greet us along the way. We learned during our trip preparations that we could not drive in the evening to the site because of the livestock on the road, and also that the crime of hitting an animal on the road is very serious in that country.

When we travelled late to the site, we were forced to sleep over in Bloemfontein. It was quite an experience. I also learned that in Lesotho, if a person commits a crime they are taken to the community chief. That is taken very seriously as it is deemed as bringing shame onto the family and family name. We received great respect from the community members within the Mokhotlong area. Workwise, I was surrounded by people with lots of industrial experience and they were very open to sharing it. They made it easy for me as a new entrant into the company. The company culture was work, work and work. We were working on a flexible time schedule though there were hours that we were required to be at the office. You had to manage your time well, meaning you had to be disciplined and make sure you delivered your deliverables on time. You had to drive your work schedule while making sure you delivered on time and yet maintaining a great relationship with other disciplines: electrical and instrumentation engineers, process engineers, the drawing office, project controls and project managers. The work was interdependent and one had to get services from these different departments. A good relationship was key to securing a timely, quality service from these other disciples.

My second site exposure was in Botswana. The people there are extremely friendly. They greet you every time they see you. A person can greet you in the morning when having breakfast at 05:00, again at the project planning meeting at 06:00 and again when you meet the person on site after the meeting. Every time they meet you they greet you, no matter how many times they've met you before. It was my first time to be in a team of engineers that had studied abroad. About 95% of the engineers on the project had studied abroad: the UK, Asia, Australia, and so on. It was quite interesting to learn such in a country that has invested so much in the education of its people, and also to learn that every second person has a farm, either farming beef or chickens, even though they have a water scarcity challenge as a country. (By nature, I take in a lot of water. They used to say they would not invite me to their houses because they would need an extra borehole for me!)

Also, I was surprised at the level of safety in the country. One could walk long distances at night without being scared of being mugged, cellular phones taken, being killed or raped. It was foreign to me as someone who lived in Khayelitsha and lost my phone while travelling to work one morning. Luckily I had not been harmed.

Working on site had its moments. We worked 06:00 to 18:00 as well as weekends and, sometimes after we had knocked off and had just left the site, we would receive a call that a particular part of the plant was not working and the production had to stop. That meant the mine would lose time on production and miss production targets, which would impact their revenue generation. We would have to go back to the site and work until the issue had been fixed. There was a night that we worked until 02:00. We were very wet and dirty as we were working on a slime line. We did not even know what time we would go home, so we needed to be disciplined, and be task-focused and -orientated.

I had the opportunity to work in historic areas in the mining industries and build relationships in the process. I am still in contact with them even now, as a relationship-building person. Botswana is one of the great countries on the African continent. It has an Eastern Cape feel, meaning that you travel between a lot of villages along the road, and you could stop the car without fear of being mugged and ask questions when getting lost and people would direct you, and you would feel very safe while travelling. One can wish that this can happen in our lovely country: that we could travel and live freely without fear. You could leave your room open, go to the site and work without fear of losing your belongings because no one would come into your room without your permission and take your belongings. You could literally leave your room wide open, go socialise in the construction camp and you would find your belongings the way they were and your room in the same state.

Travelling to Botswana was very easy and free, however there were times when I experienced working with people who did not have a sense of urgency at all and they would work at their own pace no matter how in a hurry you were. You had to learn to be patient and accommodate them. If you were like this in South Africa where I work, you would not survive for long.

This is part of working in a different country, where you also learn that it is not that easy to be in a foreign land. Our appetites, interests and priorities are very different with different working cultures. For example, workwise, in Botswana, if you are going to work on a Saturday and you plan with the local contractors to do so, do not be surprised to be alone on site. To them, Saturday is their time so they do not expect to be at work.

They will not say, "No, we are not coming." They will say, "We are coming," but they will not pitch at all! On Monday they will come with lots of excuses. Here in South Africa, contractors would not do that. If they are required to be at work they will come to work, even to the extent that some may come even if they are under the influence of alcohol, as it is a weekend. But with contractors from Botswana, the weekend is their time, so one needs to manage the work schedule with proper planning and excellent execution to try to minimise work spilling over to the weekend.

More happily, now and then you find monkeys visiting you for food. We used to say, "We have visitors!" They would come and grab food and run away. While working you could see wild animals and appreciate nature, which was a really great experience.

My third foreign working experience was in Burkina Faso. This was one of the most well organised travelling trips I have ever ventured into, when I was selected to be part of the commissioning team. I was given an introductory travelling document. It tells you what you need to do before travelling, such as get medical check-ups and vaccinations. I am a fearless person by nature. I was travelling alone on this trip to go and work with people who I had never seen and talked to: a team of engineers from Australia. That did not frighten me. I was looking forward to serving and learning. On the way to Burkina Faso I travelled via the Johannesburg–Senegal route and landed in Senegal just after 02:00. When I landed at the airport I was welcomed with an unusual experience: the workers were soldiers carrying all kinds of guns. The minute you have offloaded everything, you have to wait for the 06:00 flight to Burkina Faso.

The Senegalese are dark and very tall people. When I had just landed, I collected my luggage and was welcomed by these tall guys who said they offer accommodation because waiting until 06:00 would be long and so forth. I thought of taking them up on the offer but when they showed me the accommodation I declined as it looked very shady. I had to wait at the airport, where I discovered how free people are when practicing their beliefs. While you are standing in a queue, someone can suddenly kneel and worship their god without any fear. It was a shock for me because it is not something I had experienced before. The flight was delayed and we ended up leaving just before 08:00. It shocks your system a bit when you arrive at these African airports. Poverty is written all over the walls and you get welcomed by soldiers carrying huge guns. You think, "Am I in a war or still travelling?"

I landed in Burkina Faso and my travelling guide was there. By the grace of the Lord there was no communication challenge. At times you meet locals who can't speak English and only understand French. It was cooking hot around 10:00 – the temperatures were at a staggering 38°. I stood there soaked with sweat, wanting to get to site and eager to meet my team of people, whom I had never met. I arrived on site in the late afternoon after travelling for almost six hours on a very small tar road, often passing a roadblock of soldiers, speaking an unknown language. Every time I travel, before I land in a particular country I pray for covering and protection and thank God for carrying me through. Every time just before the flight lands, I begin to pray. However, in Burkina Faso I prayed literally every few minutes.

I was anxious yet excited and looking forward to learning and growing as an engineer and serving. We eventually arrived on site. Usually on site there is a security company patrolling the place but it was a different story in Burkina Faso. At the gate there were soldiers. You sign in with their assistance and when you finally arrive you get your room keys and try to get oriented. Besides that, it was one of the best sites I have ever worked at. The work ethic was on another level.

The Australians have no knock-off time. They work until what was scheduled for the day is carried out but when they are finished, they socialise as if they are not working the following day. They go to bed in the early hours. When I woke up at 04:00 (as we started working at 06:00), they were already up. When they get on site they work as if it is their last day of work.

The site accommodation was under the patrol of the soldiers because they were protecting us from the extremists. You would be walking to the canteen around 05:00 and bump into a huge, tall guy carrying a big gun. You get to site in office containers, you have soldiers patrolling. While you are working, the soldier is standing or walking around the office speaking a language that you do not understand. The environment requires a strong mind but it was a great site. The locals are always welcoming.

It was embarrassing to say, "I am from South Africa," as I travelled during the xenophobia season. It was a very bad one – people were burned in that one. They were asking me questions: how do we feel about this as a country, why are we so bad, how can we burn a human being? They were saying they are scared of coming to South Africa after such scenarios. The worst part is we always receive a great reception from these countries. They treat us with great respect and honour.

My first assignment onsite after induction was to be given a team of locals to work with installing piping. They couldn't speak a word of English. I had to be very creative to communicate with them to make sure they could carry out the work appropriately. It is such challenges that bring out creativity. They would say they understand but then do the opposite. To save their jobs one had to protect them. I had to use sign language and scratch on the ground with fingers to explain the drawing as they could not read drawings.

Now you are forced to be hands on so you literally have to be part of everything that needs to be done. You cannot even leave them to work independently because when you come back you will be very surprised in a bad way at what you will see. The temperatures were scorching hot. You wake up in the morning and already it is 25° at 05:00. Around 10:00, the temperature reaches 47°. You have to literally carry water to keep yourself hydrated. The mine was based in a very traditional village, still doing things in the old ways: sowing fields, using yoked cows, the wife leading them while the husband is driving, sowing whatever needed to be sowed. They live in round grass houses (oonqguphantsi). When you are inside those houses you cannot stand. You have to bend all the time when walking. The girls get married at a very early tender age, at the age of 11 they are married. It was a disturbing tradition and cultural way of doing things.

Suppliers were based in the USA and this was a critical piece of equipment to the plant because the plant could not work when this part was off line. When it stopped the whole production stopped. We had to get the supplier from the USA to come and fix it themselves, and also another team of engineers from Canada to offer a second opinion on the same piece of the equipment. Both the Americans and Canadians arrived on site at the same time – 14:00. They had to work separately because we wanted to get different opinions on the issue. They worked right through the night. When we arrived on site the following day at 06:00, the guys were still working, they worked right through until we knocked off at 18:00 when the plant could be back online. They literally did not sleep for two days working in scorching temperatures.

One of the lessons is, when the local person has passed on, the whole community and the mines must mourn for the loss, meaning the mine will shut down for the mourning period. They mourned for seven days. They wanted us not to work and for the plant to stand still for seven days as they mourned for the passing of the community member. That took a lot of negotiations between the mine and the chief. Eventually, we were allowed for the work to continue, although on the day of the funeral we had to stop working until the burial was over as a burial and mourning is something that is very important to them. While working onsite we had water breaks for people to go and get water. People would hide on the plant structure's shades. It was one of the most memorable experiences. To survive in such an environment one had to be strong mentally.

When your cellphone is not working, you have to get a local sim card, which comes with risks of being scammed by people trying to steal your money. We were not allowed to withdraw cash because it is not safe, but that did not really have an impact on us because we were in the bundus. Travelling from where the mine was to the city took more than six hours. So you only saw the city on your arrival and when you left the country. It is an experience that I will never forget. I am grateful to God for such opportunities.

* * *

One of the things about me is that I love travelling. By the grace of the Lord I have been able to travel to the following destinations for either work, religious interest or leisure: Lesotho, Thailand, Botswana, Burkina Faso, Jordan, Israel and Palestine, travelling through the following countries: Senegal, Ghana, Egypt and the Ivory Coast. These journeys have created a platform for me to learn about different cultures, religions, tribes, ethnicities, people, food, art and environment. My travelling experience has shaped me for the better and taught me to look at life differently and be grateful. These journeys also taught me to appreciate my country more. South Africa is a beautiful place and there is no better place than the place called home. Whatever country you go to, to get the best out of it, relationships are key. Even if you do not get the best reception you should always fight the good fight: the fight of building relationships.

Thailand was great for relaxing. I got days to sleep the whole day undisturbed, not worrying about anything. I also had days dedicated to touring. My phone was off for 12 days so I was shut off from everything. Having time to myself with no social media or internet connection. I could also enjoy another favourite hobby: eating! Botswana remains a choice country if I had to choose a country to live in within the African continent. This is because of the peace and the texture that country has which resembles my birthplace, especially the rurality in certain parts of the country (after all, I am a rural boy born in the valleys and mountains of the Eastern Cape, where I owe my being). Travelling gives you experiences that no one can give you and nothing can take those experiences away from you. There were scary moments in these journeys, especially in Burkina Faso. Plus there were joyous moments where I was, like, "Even if I wake up in Heaven I would not mind as this would have been the greatest send off," especially in Thailand and Israel.

THINGS FOR YOU TO THINK ABOUT:

1. Which countries have you travelled to?
2. What were the best experiences in terms of culture, environment, religion?
3. What are the challenges you encountered?
4. If you had to choose another country to live in besides your current country, which country would you choose and why?
5. What are some travelling tips that you can give based on your travelling experiences?

Chapter Nineteen
Be an agent of change

I KNOW IT HAS BECOME a popular philosophy that unfortunately sounds trite when you say it, but I do believe that we should be the change we want to see in our communities. To be authentic to this belief, I combined my interest in entrepreneurship with my goal to help foster social change by becoming a social entrepreneur. I have always been passionate about youth development and development as a whole hence I started a community soccer club at an early age. The drive was triggered by my development passion. On completion of my studies, in my early stages of work, I decided to give back to the community. Alikho Mbulana and I contacted each other, shared the vision and we were both sold to give back to the community.

In 2010, we started the Career Exhibition at Nyanga High School in the Eastern Cape, birthed from our personal experience of only finding out on the first day of university that the course I was registered for would not lead me to become an auto mechanic (though this turned out to be the best for me). I wanted to make a difference in the lives of learners in the Eastern Cape and expose them to different career opportunities and the requirements of each career. In addition to career information, we collected application forms from tertiary institutions and bursary forms from companies for the learners. We helped them apply to different institutions and made sure the learners would not be left stranded in a new city, as had happened to my friends and myself when we first went to Cape Town. This programme was effective and assisted many learners. We extended this programme to youth in Khayelitsha churches working with Luthando Mzilikazi. My wife and I also hosted many young people in our home trying to improve their lives through motivational talks and sharing our journeys with them.

My major breakthrough was in 2014, when I co-founded Waumbe Youth Development with Delphino Machikicho. This organisation has grown tremendously over the years. "Waumbe" is a Swahili word that means "empower them". Waumbe Youth Development is a registered non-profit organisation located in Fisantekraal, an informal farming community near Durbanville, situated in the northern suburbs of Cape Town. Waumbe aims and seeks to progressively develop purpose-driven African youth and equip them for the future. We started operating from the boot of a car. It was not easy at first. The Fisantekraal High School where we initially worked did not immediately capture the vision and therefore could not provide adequate support. It was not easy for us, we sacrificed our time and limited resources to be at the school but at times the learners were not organised and we would just be told to work with the available handful. They did not understand the sacrifice we made to be there, as our task teams are made up of varsity learners with limited resources to get to where we worked. It cost them time and money. However, we did not become despondent. Our motto when planting a seed was that we must plant the seed in whatever soil is presented to us. That is still our motto when we have events and do not get the audience we have anticipated. We always console ourselves with that. We make it a point we are intentional in our sessions; we do not do wishy-washy, we call them "espresso-strong coffee". What is important on our side is to show up and do the best we can with regards to what we can control and not to worry much about what we cannot control (although of course, we are concerned).

So, it has not been an easy ride at all but we have been graced by people who work from the heart. They give it their all and they are passionate about youth development so we all breathe some youth development passion. Some of our success is due to the fact that we have people sharing common goals, who came with experience of working in the youth development space. Apart from sharing common goals and experience these are the people who have gone through the same challenges that the youth is going through so they can relate.

Above all, we owe our success to the love we have for each other. We are a relationship-based organisation. We are youth in partnership with other youth to create a solution for young people. We are youth for the youth.

***

One of the major challenges we had was funding. Funders do not fund ideas; they fund tangible solutions. We had to present tangible solutions to the donors and funders before they would partner with us. Our breakthrough came from the late Robbie Gow-Kleinshmidt from Asset. He introduced us to Martje from Stichting Projecten Zuid-Afrika as a potential funder. Robbie said Martje was in the country from the Netherlands and he arranged for us to meet up with her. We had to travel more than 300km from Cape Town to get to where she was. We drove with only enough petrol to get to the destination, and none for the return trip. My younger sister, Zikhona, was so kind to fund that return trip.

They say that assumptions are dangerous and here is why I am in agreement with that sentiment. When my associate, Delphino, and I arrived at the meeting, I assumed Derek Joubert and Martje were a married couple. We pitched to them and Martje asked us a lot of questions. It felt like an interrogation. I then asked Derek where the person we were scheduled to meet was and he said, "Here, sitting with me." I froze for a second like, hmm, assumptions are dangerous. All along I thought we were just talking to a couple. Then it turned out that it is not a couple but rather Derek connecting us to a potential funder.

We were so hungry at that meeting as we had had nothing to eat on the road. If they did not offer us something to eat I wonder what would have happened. They invited us for a late lunch. When we arrived at the restaurant, Derek asked us to order. We made it a point that we would only pretend we were looking at the menu because we did not want to order first as we did not know his budget for the meeting. We told ourselves we would use his order as our guide. We would order exactly what he ordered or something in his order price range, more or less to protect his budget plan. He ordered and we said we would have the same. Now I crossed my fingers! I wondered how big the meal was as I was so starving. To my surprise, the meal was such a generous serving that I got filled up by just looking at it!

The moral of the story here: when you are invited by the client for coffee or a meal, you should simply order something in the range of the client, not order a three course meal when the client is having a burger. That is not good manners and it is inconsiderate.

We received our first funding as an organisation from that meeting. We have grown and now our resources are 55% donor reliant. The plan is to continue decreasing the donor-reliant funding percentage annually so that we can be self-sustainable.

***

In 2015, Waumbe conducted a community study in collaboration with Won Life. The goal of the study was to have a clear understanding of community challenges and identify the causes of poor academic performance and the high numbers of high school learner drop-outs. From this study, the results indicated the following factors:
- lack of career guidance
- poor academic performance
- poor health and lack of education programmes
- lack of role models from the community
- social decay

Based on the study, Waumbe's current goal is to implement programmes that progressively address the above factors by addressing the root causes of the identified challenges. These programmes aim to encourage and motivate the learners and the youth to strive for excellence in their lives despite the challenges they might be facing within their families and society. Environments of broken relationships, alcoholism, substance abuse, domestic violence and poverty are a daily reality for most of these youths.

Waumbe has developed over 10 000 youth in this community through academic development programmes such as tutoring, career guidance and tertiary application drives. Through these interventions, the only high school in the community has improved its matric pass rate from 44% in 2014 to 77% in 2021. Over 70 youth are now in 2020 formally enrolled in tertiary institutions across South Africa. This is a big boost from the starting point of less than five youths being in tertiary institutions in 2014. Waumbe facilitates youth employment to more than 75 young people annually.

The organisation has also managed to develop from being 100% donor-reliant to generating over 30% of its annual income from internal revenue streams. Waumbe owns a multipurpose youth centre that generates rental income with a number of other organisations making use of the facility. There is an internet cafe that serves the entire Fisantekraal population with internet, printing and other IT services. In 2019, the organisation became accredited to offer IT courses for youth in the community. The organisation employs five full-time staff members and 20 volunteers. I have been fortunate in that my journey in social entrepreneurship is decorated by multiple awards and accomplishments.

***

To become a successful social entrepreneur, I learned that I had to be hard-working. Unlike having a job, you are on your own. If you do not do what needs to be done, nobody will. It was tough but it is getting better although every year presents different opportunities and challenges. There are times when I pray, sleep, and wake up praying, and talking alone and not answering calls. I am not really an anxious person by nature. I just feel back and shoulder pains, and then I try to find out what is bothering me.

If I did not manage to go crazy in August 2018, I will never go crazy. When we got our first ever opportunity to facilitate a learnership programme, we took it for granted that it was going to be easy: the Waumbe centre renovations would be complete by the time the programme was due to start and we would have ticked all the necessary boxes. We needed to get the centre fully fledged, renovated and disabled-user friendly. I was, like, "We will get all these things sorted. We will be ready at the planning meeting in July." The programme was going to kick off in August 2018. The renovation costs escalated and we had a budget shortfall of R126 000, and we needed the centre ready before 1 August. My strength comes from the Lord and everything I am and have is through Him. Two weeks before the project kicked off and with outstanding work and a huge shortfall. I got home and asked everyone who was in the house to come and pray, and so we prayed. Boom!

The following day around midday, I received an email from Stichting Projecten Zuid-Afrika saying they had sent our request for funding to King Baudouin Foundation and King Baudouin Foundation confirmed that they would assist us. My day was made. I just thanked God.

After that, half of the problem was solved. Another problem was the recruitment for the learnership programme of 43 young people living with disabilities. We put out an advert and I thought things would be easy as a pie. To my surprise, things did not work out until the day of the programme kick-off. On that day, everything just fell into place. The client was screaming in my ears over the phone. When the client called it was like a hot hairdryer on your ears. I was, like, "I have never succumbed to that pressure." If I was a smoker, I would have smoked weed that day or a whole packet of cigarettes! It was tough. The worst part about that particular project was that we were not really going to get paid for it. We were playing our part with regard to unemployment eradication. Think of Romans 8.28: "And we know that in all things God works for the good of those who love him, who have been called according to his purpose." As witnessed on that day in August, everything was spot on. We were able to deliver to the client: the centre was ready, the facilitators were ready and the learners were ready, and we had an induction. If I did not have my heart towards community development, I would have said to the client, "Please hike the mountain," as the situation was unbearable.

I did not need this kind of pressure in my life. I slept with my eyes wide and woke up with my eyes wide open. I conquered this because of resilience and commitment, because when I have put my mind to something I do not back down. Though this one nearly left me with grey hair. How do I retreat from such a situation? First, through a smile when seeing the project actually take off and, second, by thanking everyone involved in pulling it through. I believe in the saying that goes "If you want to go fast, go alone; if you want to go far, go together." I always have people around me. I am surrounded by a team of brilliant individuals who make sure we always cross the line with flying colours – the likes of Ncebakazi Mabhena, Curt van Schalkwyk, Nombuso Mazibuko, then Lwando Mzoyi and, now, Asiphe Khemtse and Moses Lefora. This is the winning team, even if we win with wounds. Also, I have people who believe in me and support me all the way, and they look at me critically and when they say no, they do so with love. We trust each other's judgement. I celebrate the success with the team over brunch and I have my coffee with cheesecake.

***

Entrepreneurship is a cold, lonely road and every hour counts. If the hour passes without doing work that can be invoiced, that means there will be no money made that hour. If all my hours in that particular month were not spent doing work that could be billed, it would mean there would be no revenue for the enterprise in that month. The invoice you have in your hands might be the last one for that season. There are no guarantees in this journey; no one owes you anything.

I also believe that vision interpretation is everything. For example, if the Waumbe vision was misinterpreted, the organisation would not be here today. We need young people who have the heart to share their visions with the right and appropriate people and be willing to learn patiently. I had to be patient even though the vision was burning inside of me, as it took six months to be interpreted from the date I met Mr Isaacs, who assisted in interpreting the vision from September 2013 to March 2014.

It is also very important to believe in your idea and be consistent. However, planning and excellent execution is key. Many organisations start out very well but then they begin to fizzle out. This sector is difficult but you have to keep doing what you do best. Results do not come easy but you have to continue working. I always tell my team, "We need to work as if someone is watching us, for we never know who is." Consistency is key, as is always showing up when you have promised to show up even if you do not feel like it at times.

There is also great value in praying for what you believe in, in being a spiritual individual. I feel that for me to be able to remain calm in difficult periods, I need to pray. Another important element to succeed as a social entrepreneur is the ability to network. For Waumbe to be successful, the organisation has developed multiple partnerships to support the project in various ways. One of the key partnerships for Waumbe is with universities in the Western Cape. Our ability to network has allowed the organisation to partner with a number of these institutions. This is a skill that I developed early in life when I needed to build relationships to survive.

As I mentioned earlier in the book, mentorship is an important part of any person's life. Without my leadership mentor Mr Jannie Isaacs and spiritual mentor Pastor Vanya, I would not be where I am today. I have learned a lot from them, as they have walked this journey of leadership before me.

THINGS FOR YOU TO THINK ABOUT:

1. Are you perhaps part of a game changer organisation?
2. How did you become part of it?
3. What is your organisation doing?
4. If not part of it now would you consider being part of it in any form?

Chapter Twenty

Take increasingly bigger steps to prepare for your great endeavour

THIS BOOK IS INSPIRED by my journey in running.

The story of this book all began when my family and I were on our way from the Eastern Cape in 2017. Ezekiel was five years old then. We stopped in Knysna for lunch. He ordered sushi for his lunch and I was, like, I will watch and see and to my surprise he knew all about it and he ate all of it. While we were waiting for the meals, he then said, "Dad, I had a dream. I saw you having a book and signing an autograph for a long queue of people buying the book."

Then the idea was refuelled in 2019 while we were in Israel for a tour travelling with a family friend, Dr Junia Murori. We were discussing the technicalities of running races: that it is not just about running; it's a journey that is a lot more than just running. She said this is so rich it needs to be documented. Actually, Dr Moruri is the one who gave the book the name *The Conquering Spirit* at Jerusalem Gold Hotel after listening to the journey of running and also the work I do.

* * *

My eldest brother introduced me to long-distance running as a sport. He came to Cape Town to run the Two Oceans Marathon in 2015, and I transported him to the race starting point and picked him up from the finishing point afterwards.

"Next year you must run as well," he said. In January 2016, he reminded me again. He went ahead and got me registered and all that so I started training then. That was my first time running in a proper race ever. My first race was the Kloof Nek Classic 21km, 31 January 2016. I finished the race in 1:33. I did not train for more than 14kms before I undertook the race. I was just running without awareness, as I was not even aware of running times, the cut off times, and I basically knew nothing about running.

I just ran.

After the Kloof Nek, I entered to run the Two Oceans Marathon. I also ran it without training for more than 14km. I finished the race in 4:57. My brother was shocked when he realised that I crossed the line before him.

"How did you do it?" he asked me.

"I just ran. That is all," I said.

I ran all my races without awareness or an understanding of preparation, the diet, the cut-off times and so forth. I was simply running. Then, in November 2017, I met Melikhaya Nkumanda Peteni (Stallion, I call him Stally), who I was always running behind at the races, which is what made me take notice of him. I asked him where he trains and he offered to train with me. We decided that we would begin training together in 2018. We started training together at the beginning of February. I used to go pick him up in the morning around 04:30 for training. He was staying in Dunoon, one of the townships in Cape Town. However, that life of training together was cut short due to safety concerns because robbers use that time of the morning to target people. His family was once robbed during that time. The robbers noticed that he was leaving around that time and went to rob his family while he was out. Also, it was not safe for me, though I was driving. I kept the car ready to fly should there be any awkward movement. When I noted a group of shady people walking towards me, I would move the car slowly to be ready to take off. Anyway, during that short season of training together, he taught me about a runner's personal best, running nutrition and that there is sub 3 in marathon running that I did not know about. The first marathon I ran with more insight on how to prepare and pace myself was the Cango Cave Marathon in Oudtshoorn in 2018. We ran this race together as partners and we were pacing each other to the finish line. I completed the marathon in 2:56 and he crossed the line in 2:57, just behind me. From then my journey in running changed. I am a sub 3 marathon runner. When my brother saw how much I had improved, he said I was ready to run the Comrades and urged me to enter the race. This was much earlier than I'd scheduled. My plan was always to run a Comrades Marathon after five years of running but he said, "You are ready now." I entered but unfortunately I was involved in a car accident three months before the race and I could not train. I started training a week before the Comrades. Actually, I wanted to pull out due to lack of training but my brother said, "Go for the experience."

Once again, I ran a race without proper preparation but still being in recovery from an accident injury. It was quite a life-teaching journey. You get all kinds of complications: you get sick, chest pains and all that. What I did was to pray and ask God to heal me along the journey when these uncomfortable experiences kicked in. When I was at 60km, I met a woman called Cathy who was running for Sunninghill Running Club and we ran together for about 17km and then she started to slow down. I also slowed down because we were partners now and I felt that she contributed to my journey.

She asked me a question: "Why are you slowing down?"

I told her, "I am waiting for you."

She said I must go on. If I did not, I would miss the silver time. I did not want to go at first. She then said, "Please go. I will cost you silver if you wait for me."

I decided to go when I was at 85km. There was a guy standing next to the road and he said to me, "My guy, you are eligible for the silver medal. Please, please push harder." I pushed very hard and I completed my race just in time to squeeze in a silver medal at 7:29. The cut off time is 7:30.

During my second Comrades Marathon I was again hammered by an ITB (Iliotibial band syndrome) injury this time, so said my physiotherapist. I pulled a muscle while doing my last long-run training session for the race. It happened on 1 May 2019, as I was running a 78km training distance. Somehow I felt uncomfortable at 40km.

That is when I realised that there was something wrong with my leg. I continued the run despite this, which was naughty of me, because I should have stopped at 40km when I felt uncomfortable. I managed to run until I finished the 78km run. After that 78km long training, there was a 50km tempo run on 8 May 2019. I attempted to do it, but I had to pull out at 40km because the pain was unbearable and my other leg was being negatively affected. I went to a physiotherapist to try to get a fix for the leg problem in time for the Comrades Marathon but I was only cleared to run on Thursday of that week by my physio, Luan Wakefield, one of the best physios in the city. The Comrades was going to take place on Sunday meaning I only had two days of training before the marathon. I only managed to squeeze in a 5km training run to test my legs after I was cleared, and after that I went to run the Comrades. The key to success in these races is the management of the psychology of a race. Physical strength also has to be managed very well. I crossed the finish line at 7:23, which was a six-minute improvement from my first Comrades in 2018. It was a psychological battle, because physically my abilities were limited and it was an uprun, which tests your strength.

***

Running is like a life journey. You can have all the ingredients to succeed in life, but if you are not strong psychologically and mentally, those ingredients for success will be in vain. This book has been inspired by overcoming through the conquering spirit, which is inherently stored within us. Running introduced me to another form of life and experience that I was not aware of. Running humbles you. You can train and be fit as an iron, but come race day, things might turn out for the worst. Training hard does not guarantee good results; it gives you an opportunity to give your best shot. Every race is unpredictable; you have to remain humble because every race will show you different kinds of flames. You need grace for every race; you cannot conclude that you will do better than in the previous race, as everything depends on the race day. You might get sick, you might get injured, or you might mismanage your fitness on the day. Anything can happen. The best way I describe the race day outcome is: if God permits, I will do well. Such is life. Life humbles you. You can have all the degrees from the best universities and not really achieve much in life. The definition of success depends on the person; the way I describe success is totally different to the next person. So what success means to me is totally different to what success means to another person. As the saying goes, beauty is in the eye of the beholder.

The 2020 and 2021 Comrades Marathons were cancelled because of the coronavirus pandemic and the associated requirements for everyone to practice social distancing to curb the spread of the virus. However, I am hopeful that 2022 will happen as normal, and I am trusting in God that I will accomplish 6 hours and 30 minutes, which would be a 53-minute improvement.

Running has a community of caring people who offer other runners great support. When you run, you meet many people along the road cheering for you, giving you the necessary support. Besides cheering you on, they give you food and so forth. They are there to ensure that you succeed in your race plans, even though they do not know your race plan for the day. They are just there to support you no matter how big or small your dreams are for the race. Also, runners help each other along the route when they are having difficulties. Some will even stop and ask you how you are and how they can assist, even though they have never met you before, mind you. If you still have some fight in you, they offer to continue the run together, even though they do not know your name, or even ask for it. They put their running destinies on hold for a second to make it a point you do well on the day. They even go as far as sharing their nutrients to ensure that you are well taken care of.

* * *

Running instils the need for preparation, diligence and maintenance in your life: it enforces discipline and a culture of hard work. Runners work very hard and make a lot of sacrifices along the way. Running is not easy at all. No one gets used to it. Every time one gets onto the road it is different. We have running coaches who give us training programmes and we follow their advice. The coach is at liberty to discipline us if we do not adhere to the programme and plans. On the race day, you have to stick to the race plan and diet. Race day is not a good day to experiment with your diet: you do not eat what you have never eaten before, as it can create problems during the race.

While running, do not get influenced by what other people are doing; stick to your pace and race plan no matter how tempting it is to follow the flow. Some of the people are not there to finish the marathon, they are pacers who are in the race to pace a specific person for a measured duration of time and distance, trying to assist that particular runner to achieve the race objectives. After that they will leave that person at the distance they have agreed to. So, if you get carried away because of their pace and follow them, you will be in trouble as you will have wasted your capacity to run longer with a quality time. Discipline is key and sticking to your pace. Such is life. You have to stick to your life plan and your pace and not get carried away by those in close proximity. Also, along the route, you will meet people who express their belief in you. They will give you words of encouragement, such as, "You can do it!" and "Keep going. You're almost there." Even when doubts begin because of the toughness of the journey, they fuel you and make you believe once again. Such is also needed in life, because the going can get very tough. Life is hard and can be messy at times. We need people along the path of life that will encourage us along the road and make us believe once again.

***

Like in work or personal relationships, you also meet people who will discourage you. I remember my third Two Oceans Marathon, which is 56km long. I was chasing a silver medal. In order to get it, one has to finish the race in under four hours. I mispaced myself in the process and burned myself. When I was at Constantia Nek, I met a group of people. They said, "He is tired as hell!" (using one of the popular Xhosa swear words). Instead of motivating me, they swore at me and they themselves could not even finish 2km running at the pace I was running. I missed the silver medal by 17 minutes, crossing the line at 4:17. The Two Oceans is one of the toughest but greatest ultramarathons, because of the road profile. However, I eventually got the silver medal in 2019, crossing the finish line at 3:57. This remains one of my memorable moments in the running fraternity, and is also my highlight in running thus far.

Words are a most powerful weapon. In one of my races – during my second Cango Caves Marathon Race in 2019 – I was exhausted around 12km before the finish line. The race was hard because I had not trained for it as well as I would have preferred because of an injury.

My coach, Bethuel M. Lephallo, said, "You should just go and enjoy the race," and he continued, "You can do it."

I kept thinking that – "I can do it" – when the going got tough.

He believed in me even when my body said it could not go any further. I normally pray a lot as I run the route and that gives me strength. Prayers and the words of encouragement from my coach before the race are always instrumental on the day.

The words stuck with me to the finish line, with a race time of 2:49. My current personal best for a marathon (42.2km) is 2:38, which is a pace of 3 minutes and 48 seconds per kilometre; my half-marathon (21.1km) personal best is 1:14 (3min27sec per km); my 10km personal best is 0:32 (3min17sec per km), and my Ultra Marathon 56km personal best is 3:57. I have also improved my Comrades Marathon time from 7:29 in 2018 to 7:23 in 2019 – a six-minute improvement on an uprun.

* * *

Running is a way of life. It is a great analogy for life itself because a runner must have a conquering spirit, held up by leadership, relationships, faith, perseverance and passion.

You may have noticed that there are three common things that we battle within a race that we also battle with in life: the battles are psychological, physical and mental.

During a race, when running, my body says, "I cannot do it anymore". Then the mental and psychological strength needs to kick in to keep me moving forward. My experience has taught me that I succeed because I manage these elements well.

And, as always, it's the relationships that form the foundation of everything. On my "team" I have a family that supports me: my running teammates (my Team Just Run family); the technical team that analyses previous runs and plans and sets targets for my upcoming races with my coach, Bethuel; and my manager, TK Mhelembe, who is always there strategising for my races. He is very supportive and loves sport in general. The way he serves is phenomenal; he will wake up early in the morning to support us when training to supply the nutrients along the route while we run. Also, as always, I have my family behind me. My mother wakes up on race days to watch me on races that are televised. My wife and sons share me with the road. So I have a lot of supporters along the journey of running. In life we need this kind of support because life can be ruthless, especially the detours, the uphills and the battles.

There have always been people with me on my journey. My family has been there through thick and thin; they know and understand me better than anyone. I am stubborn at times. They could have easily given up on me, but they are there even at times when they do not understand and feel what I feel, and I appreciate them though I might not say it now and again. They have been a pillar of strength.

Finally, the Lord has been very faithful in my race through life. There is no season of my life that the Lord has not provided for.

* * *

Things for you to think about:

1. What has been your strategy in your life goals?
2. How did you overcome it when facing uphill battles towards your journey of success?
3. What has been instrumental in your life journey?
4. Who has played a crucial role on the road to success?
5. What keeps you grounded?

Endorsements

Siyabulela Luzipho, friend

My journey with Mdumiseni wasn't the typical rural boy's experience. Ours was rather more adventurous. We grew up mostly in the forest and mountains hunting. I remember one time we were hunting and saw a snake. It attacked me first but Mdu fought it off and risked his life because he is a good man and always was.

Among the boys we grew up with he was one of the smartest and kindest. He always thought ahead and didn't like fighting even though he was a good fighter. He liked football very much.

Life was not good during those days for us as we were both raised by parents who hadn't gone to school so where they worked they got minimum wage. When there was no food at my home, Mdu would share his plate with me as I did in return.

In the early years, our parents and grandparents taught us to look after livestock, as well as farming. If we were not in the mountains you would probably find us working the yellow soil of Mthozela.

As years went by, we became teenagers and we were growing towards manhood, which meant fending for our families. In those days, there were two options: going to work in the mines or going to school. Mdu and I were no longer young naive rural boys but had to go into the big world to further our studies. I moved to Cape Town for high school and he went to a boarding school. We've stayed friends ever since.

Songezo Libala, junior school classmate

I met Mdumiseni in 1995, we went to the same school (Chokomfeni Junior Secondary School) in Qumbu Mthozela Location. We were in the same class. We were both doing Standard 5, which is now called Grade 7. He and his sister Ntombevesi used to sell snacks at school. He was very strict and never wanted to give us any credit. He was a very quiet and focused learner, and he was a hard worker of note and did his schoolwork with diligence. He was never one to make noise in the classroom, but would never snitch on anyone when the teachers wanted to find out who was making noise. We were in the same school for three years and I don't remember him getting into trouble or his parents being called to the school.

Phumezo Myataza (KO), high school friend

I met this oke early in 1998 briefly when I came to high school. We were there till 2000. So I had the privilege of staying with him in 2000 at Nyanga High School. We became acquaintances and we were doing matric at the time. Now, if you have ever stayed in the hostel, you'd know matric is the best year (uligqala) when everyone is familiar with you and you know everything about everything around school. Mdu was a very focused and hard-working student throughout the three years at high school.

We had a boarding master at school and we called him BM (Mr Dlwathi). He appeared to hate everyone. Most guys were not quite fond of him. BM was not a bad or cruel person; he was just very strict and was teaching us the way of life. So I picked up that not only was Mdu friendly with the team that worked with BM, but BM was also fond of Mdu. He used to call him Menze. I knew, and everyone knew, it takes a perfect character to be liked by BM. Then I became friends with this gentleman after we had been separated to stay in different dormitories.

I noticed that when he woke up, he woke me up. His bed was next to mine, but at my previous dormitories we never used to do that. So I saw a caring person in him, and more so, kindliness.

As the year progressed, he took an interest in ballroom dancing and boxing. He was quite energetic and ambitious. I was also doing ballroom dancing at the time. So we used to practice our moves in the dormitory at the hostel. Sometimes I did moves carelessly. Mdu doesn't like it when you treat things carelessly. So that's how we used to practise, and at varsity he made it to championships.

We used to get the best lessons in town, needless to say. Mdu became the best and fastest-learning student there. He was focused. I remember that we used to dance as a school to go to competitions in different places and win trophies. Mdu showed us how it could be done better.

One Saturday morning, we left the hostel to town, where our rehearsals normally took place. That day, Spar Ngcobo was hosting a boxing match in front of the store. Mdu did everything to make sure that the dancers took part in that. At the time, Mdu didn't have control in the dance club or of the dancers but, just as Mdu wanted, the dancers were there to open for the boxing clubs and Mdu was one of them. He took care of everything: marketing, advertising, management, selling the idea to the dancers, promotion and leadership. And, indeed, that was one of the successful projects at eNgcobo.

As the year progressed, Mdu continued to show courage, kindliness and just peace in most of the school activities. Mdu had a family in Ngcobo town who were quite well known in the area. In the many times that we went there together, I've never seen a person that worked as hard in their home as Mdu did, and he did it willingly. I know how happy his family was when he was there. He was a very focused young man who knew what he wanted and knew that if you want something you need to work for it; his family loved that about him. These are qualities he showed even at school.

At school Mdu could mingle with almost everyone. He was a people's person. There're very few people who did not know Mdu from our school. He loved clothes and cleanliness. He was always very neat and proper, with class and style. He had a walk that said: "I am in control." You'd never miss it.

As you would know, everyone has the kind of music they like. At the time kwaito was the most popular, but I remember TKZee Family, Mandoza and Arthur. If you've never seen Mdu dance twalatsa, you've never seen kwaito. It's not your normal twalatsa. He used to kill it. I remember even when we went to varsity, he was still a great dancer. We loved kwaito too much, and more than that, we were brothers then as we still are now.

So Mdu was one of those people who could engage with people from all sorts of backgrounds, be it they are from the church, drunkards, teachers, old or young ladies, teachers and people from all walks of life. He is gifted with the ability to attract a community around him, and he brings a smile to everyone. Mdu is super ambitious, courageous, hard-working, dedicated, kind and super strong. He takes what God has granted him no matter the obstacles, come what may.

Siwiwe Tyokolo, high school and university friend

Mdu and I met at Nyanga High School where we completed our matric in the year 2000. During his high school years, Mdu was always loving, kind, humble, calm and, most importantly, focused on his studies. And he also fell in love with dance at this time. Most of my peers, including Mdu, were accepted for tertiary level education in Cape Town during 2001, when he enrolled to study towards a diploma in mechanical engineering. I, however, didn't join them in Cape Town and went to the Vaal. We kept the communication alive with Amajita during this time. Tertiary life brought about this freedom with no parents or boarding school rules. I heard a lot of stories about other peers, not bad stories though, about how they were starting to experience tertiary life (fun). But not Mdu; he kept his cool and his only focus was his education and also the love of dance, maybe because he knew where he came from. At the top of his list was wanting to change the situation back at home as most of us wanted to make life better for our parents. Even though life in tertiary wasn't easy, Mdu kept his shoulders and head high. All he was happy about at that time was that he was at Tech and studying towards his bright future. You can imagine: you left home knowing the situation and now you are in this concrete jungle with all different kind of students from different backgrounds. Most had everything that some of us wished for during those days. On the other hand, Mdu had to make a plan so life must continue.

Mdu was a people's person during those years at Tech and he knew the right people at the right places. I knew most people through him.

I joined him in 2002 and he welcomed me to his room, where he had a roommate. I was squatting with him and sharing a single bed. Ha ha! At least now life was a little better but also not better, meaning we carried each other's heavy load on our shoulders. We were even sharing clothes because we were almost the same height.

Mdu became chairperson of Tech's dance club so he had something else that kept him busy besides studies. They were travelling a lot. Even though he didn't have much at Tech, he was happy that there was a roof over his head and he made every second count. Life at Tech showed us life isn't all about what you have or have not, what your background is, but all about keeping your head up and focusing on your goals. Mdu during tertiary times was kind, humble and mostly respectful to everyone.

Vuyo Menze, older brother

Mdu is a very energetic leader: full of ideas and opinions that are well-informed by his drive for societal well-being. He's very smart, intelligent and fearless of challenges he faces.

Vuyokazi Menze, older sister

Good people, I don't know where to start when talking about my younger brother, my young lion Mdumiseni. I'm three years older than he is, but it seems as if he is the one who is older than me. He checks on me frequently. He brings me a lovely bond unlike any other and smiles in my needy moments. He brings joy and hope to my soul when I'm hurt.

He is the kind of a brother anyone would want and enjoy. He is so loving, caring, humble, inspirational, respectful and intelligent and, above all, he fears God. To me he is really a good friend and a blessing in my life.

Sukude Gxarha Khondwana Santsaba, Cikizwa Menze, younger sister

Mdu, our dear brother, is a strong man who pushes through odds when he wants to achieve something. For example, as a leader he puts the needs of his people ahead of his own and ensures they all get what they need.

He is a selfless man who loves strongly. He always wishes other people the best. For example, by helping people achieve their goals in life. Mdu is a teachable hard worker, who is obedient and down to earth.

Zikhona Menze, younger sister

Mdu is a very humble soul. He is a smart, genuine intellectual by nature. He inherited those traits from his parents. He is also mature. He loves people and his family, especially his wife and children. He also loves his church as he is a pastor.

People say he is the father to the fatherless. He has sympathy for all people regardless of their religion and culture. He always smiles, even when his heart is bleeding. He is one of the kindest.

Phelokazi Menze, younger sister

Mdumiseni Menze is the coolest brother I have: kind, loving, caring, supportive and friendly. He is always willing to listen to your problems and he will just say, "This is nothing, my angel. I have been through a lot and now listening to you, I think taking your problems to God is the best solution. Yes, it will take time for you to conquer it but trust me, I know."

He is a prayer-warrior and a God-fearing person. Last but not least, my brother loves food. Food is his best friend.

Buti, keep up what you have been doing. We are proud of you always and we love you so much.

Osca Menze, younger brother

There are a lot of things to say about my brother but I just want to say he is a good man. I mean, judging from the things he does for the community of Fisantekraal and the church he leads.

He didn't just start at that community, he started at home way before he had his own family. As he likes to say, "charity begins at home."

He has been my financial pillar since Grade 1 and I am now doing my second year at the University of Cape Town. All that is because of the motivation, blessings, guidance and his just being a brother whenever I needed one and a father if I needed one, after we lost our father.

He is a family man. One of the best fathers I have ever seen. He invests his time, mind and soul to Waumbe and as a result he works until 03:00 most of the time. He does not give up. That helps him run races.

In his house there is always a seat for anyone in need. If he cannot give you the help you need, he will get it elsewhere. His wisdom is beyond measure. The patience he has is the same as that of a predator waiting for its prey.

He listens and gives good advice. He loves and cares for everyone. He is a good father to everyone around him.

Dr Ayanda Menze, wife

I met this man in 2011 and was immediately captured by his handsome looks. I said to my friend, "He is a handsome young man, nhe?" My friend nodded in agreement. I was just making a general comment, little did I know that he was my destined husband, father of my kids and heart of my life. I call him Ntliziyo yam, to denote that he is the heart of my life. On 11 May at 15:00, we said our I dos, rehearsed the holy matrimonial promises to each other. Up to this day I have not looked back. I have so much to say about him. I can certainly compile an entire book on him.

At home he is a present husband and father, loving us to the best of his ability. The kind of husband who is involved in daily home chores, including taking time to go via grocery stores to buy monthly groceries or just to grab whatever we need at a given moment. The kind of daddy who is able to wake up from his sleep in the middle of the night to refill a baby's feeding bottle or to hunt for a misplaced pacifier (dummy; soother), a daddy who gives all his kids a bath straight from birth until they can do it independently and one who changes diapers. His favourite chore to do at home is buying lots of food for us (maybe because eating great food is also one of his hobbies; this man can eat yhey!!! Ha ha! I even have to prepare two chickens (mleqwa) sometimes, because, a whole chicken is for him, he insists!!! He says, "Food is for the stomach and the stomach is for food") and spending time taking care of his children. His downtimes are Sunday afternoons, most spent with me. We always have a Sunday lunch buffet as a family. Occasionally, he organises stolen moments away from the kids by booking a Sunday lunch for two. After lunch, he always invites me for movies. He has a great taste for great movies. I never try, because well … you can guess! Every morning he prepares to take a bath with me. He even makes a point to call me on his way from running to say, "Don't take a bath without me. Wait! I'm almost there."

He has showered me with so much love, kindness and support in the most mundane daily home routines and during the greatest and the worst of times and seasons of our union. I truly could not ask God for a better husband and could not dream of a better father for my children.

He is my personal champion; I am his greatest fan. This is because as I watch him live his daily life, I would encapsulate his entire stature/person as a champion. A champion is often defined as one who has surpassed all rivals in a sporting contest or other competition, or one who vigorously supports or defends a person or cause. These definitions are orientated towards the external and are oblivious to the rivals that arise or even exist within the champion, the internal factors within the one who defends or supports the cause. Rivals such as one's background, race, culture, level of education, mindset, insecurities, fear of the unknown, fear of failure, self-doubt and all other internal battles. My husband stands as a champion to me because his achievements surpass all these internal battles. He contends against all known limitations faced by every African child and stands strong to shine the light within his reach.

He is my champion because, in 2012, I married a young mechanical engineer who had a secure job in a mining firm. I witnessed him arise as a champion when he lost his employment through retrenchment. Instead of starting a pity party for himself, this man started his own consulting company (Intambiso), instead of blaming God the Creator for his misfortunes, he started a church (Heart of True Worship) to bring glory to the name of the Lord, instead of blaming his unfavourable background, he capitalised on his personal story and built Waumbe (an organisation that empowers the youth to grasp all opportunities within their reach no matter how hopeless their circumstances may seem), instead of dragging his feet feeling sorry for himself, he lifted his strides in marathon running and is now a Comrades silver medalist.

He is a man I look up to and learn a lot from. His backbone is his immovable faith in God as his personal saviour and redeemer, Jesus Christ. He draws his strength from his daily prayer sacrifices. His discipline and consistency in prayer and exercise is nothing I have ever experienced before. I have never seen a human being repeat the same thing, daily, at the same time.

His spiritual and physical disciplines include waking up during the early hours of the morning at 03:00, 04:00 or 05:00 daily to start by offering up prayers to God and then hit the road for a long-distance run. My husband's lifestyle reminds me of these ancient words, once spoken by Apostle Paul: "For that reason, I don't run just for exercise or boxing like one throwing aimless punches, but I train like a champion athlete. I subdue my body and get it under my control, so that after preaching the good news to others I myself won't be disqualified" (1 Corinthians: 9.26–27).

I watch him daily, in admiration as he lives a life well governed, thus I am certain of this fact: where he is now is just the beginning of his greatness.

Nkitha, Ezekiel and Emmanuel, sons

The first time I met my dad, I didn't think that I would regard him as someone I would look up to as a father because I didn't have a present father before in my life. But through these eight years I have been with him, my opinion of him has changed.

If I were to describe him with one word, I would describe him as tough. My dad works really hard, nearly every day and I rarely see him slack off. He encourages me to always do my best even though he doesn't say it as much. He works hard even in dire situations, and that's what I really admire about him. That taught me that hard times will come, so I have to be strong enough to keep going because these hard times never last.

He is a loving and caring father who respects his children. He leaves the house until in the evening so that he can provide for his family. He is also respectful of other people. As his children we love him as he loves us as his children.

Nothobile Ndyalivane, elder

One of the years I will never forget is the year I met the man of God, Mdumiseni Menze, through my children. He was doing home visits, as he normally does for the members of the church. This touched me, as I saw magnificent love. He came to my house, which is looked down on by people of his stature. He sat on my torn-apart couches. He did not sit there for a few seconds, he sat for a long time and spoke about God.

He also spoke with my children. I admired this wonderful thing he was doing. I loved watching him interact with my children and believed that this is the child of God doing a good thing. I told myself that the following Sunday I was going to attend his church for a visit. My children were so amazed by the work God did in their lives through Mdumiseni Menze! I visited the church and I could not leave it, because I saw the man of God who preaches good news; a humble man full of love and who loves the Lord.

As I started to fellowship at Heart of True Worship International Church, things changed at my house. My partner wanted nothing to do with God, but he eventually repented and accepted Jesus Christ through Mdumiseni's preaching because he saw a humble man of God. We saw God in him and his church.

We have continued our spiritual journey with him since 2018, and he has never changed since then – he is still humble and loving the Lord and all the communities. Young as he is, he taught me things I did not know. He showed up for my family, and when my husband was sick he would wake up at four in the morning and pray for him. He is not lazy – he is the father that is always hungry to help. He helps in the church and in the community. As we speak, he is the co-founder of Waumbe. When my husband passed away he was there and he is a brother to my children. He is a person who does good. May he continue loving God and be humble.

Zizo Bomali, church leader

It has been three years since I began serving under the leadership of Pastor Mdu, but even in my short time I have discovered a hard and fast truth: God is alive. I feel privileged to be part of his ministry.

Pastor Mdu is a very kind and selfless person who always goes out of his way to help people around him. He is a good listener and does not make judgements on people's situations. He makes time to interact with members of the church serving under his ministry. He is very supportive. I have never met a pastor as supportive as him.

He runs community outreaches together with his wife. He speaks with wisdom, and only when he sees a need to do so. He is very loving to his kids and family.

He taught us how to pray, and the importance and the power of prayer. He prays for everything, and does not give up in any situations. He is a God-fearing man. He is a very dedicated, ambitious and true leader. He always brings the best out of people. He leads by example. Time is very important to him – he is very punctual. He is very strong in faith; he is unshakable.

Ziyanda Nozombile, church leader

It is an honour to comment on the attributes of Pastor Mdumiseni Menze. I am happy to say it has been a great benefit to serve under his leadership at Heart of True Worship International Church and at Waumbe Youth Development Centre.

I have known Pastor Menze for four years now – from February 2016 till this day – and I feel qualified to present his qualities to you. I know him as a father, a spiritual father and a leader. His humble spirit and youth-centred leadership makes it easy to approach him.

He goes beyond limitations to serve the Church of God and the community of Fisantekraal. His consistent behaviour makes him fully established in all areas of his life. Humility and prayer are some of the outstanding qualities he has and love is his second nature.

He is very understanding. Pastor Menze filled a gap of a father figure in my life that I missed during my upbringing. He is amazing in all ways. He lives love, and that is one most important thing I would love to inherit from him.

Pastor Menze embodies all those long-lost qualities of pastors – men and leaders in our communities. If we were to live in an environment full of people of his calibre, we would not be fighting for safety and freedom as women.

Mfundo Nondyola, church leader

I've known Mdu since 2017. He is a man who is dedicated to bringing change to the community spiritually and mentally. He gives equal effort at the work of God and in the community.

He invests the most in people who have lost faith in themselves. What I mean is that he knows that time equals money, love and many things. He has lost some, and gained some but he is helping the hopeless and that is his goal.

Kele Thebe, media and marketing team leader

I have had the privilege of working with Mdu for a few years, and in this time there has never been a moment where he did not display selflessness, compassion and love for those around him.

One of the traits I admire most about Mdu is that, having seen him interact with people from all walks of life, children, Waumbe task team members, board members and members of the community, he always addresses everyone with the same level of respect.

He never misses a chance to make everyone laugh and feel welcomed. He is a true reflection of what a leader should be. His dedication to community development is very admirable and it shows in the amazing work that he does as the leader of Waumbe Youth Development.

Tshegofatso Maleka, Waumbe administration leader

Mdu is a humble man of God, who works hard to create change in the lives of those around him. His excellent interpersonal skills enable him to get along well with anyone. In addition to this, he is a very selfless man who is passionate about youth and community development. As the CEO of Waumbe Youth Development, Mdu has taken the role of a broker for many young people from Fisantekraal.

Mthobeli Lithiko, Waumbe mentorship leader

Mr Menze, or should I say Pastor Menze, or should I say my leader – I've known him for the past five years, since I joined the Waumbe Youth Development team. I very much applaud the kind of work that he does in my community – Fisantekraal.

Looking back to when Waumbe started, even before I joined the organisation, and judging by where it is now, and where it is heading to, I have to give credit to Mr Menze for all the hard work and dedication he put in to make sure that the organisation best serves its purpose in the community.

I would personally like to thank Mr Menze so much for all the hard work he is doing in my community. Keep on being the good leader that you are, and, most importantly, keep on being a great friend, brother and father to all of the people that you support on different levels. I very much enjoy your sense of humour, and all the funny memes you send us via our WhatsApp chat group.

Ida Okeyo, Waumbe education, development and innovation team leader

It has been an honour to have met and worked with Mdu for the past two years. His energy, zeal and motivation towards youth development has challenged me in many ways. It's such a privilege to be able to reflect on Mdu's work, which has inspired me and others. His dedication to Waumbe Youth Development work and other aspects of his life have been great to watch.

Delphino Machikicho, Waumbe co-founder and executive director

Coming from Zimbabwe as a young man, I had preconceived ideas about South Africa. I had watched on TV the violence, the abuse and I was worried for my life. However, Zimbabwe was going to stifle my dreams and aspirations, so I had no option.

Two doors away from my apartment there was a young man who changed my preconceived ideas of this beautiful country. He became my first South African friend. We would talk about everything as though we had known each other for life. He is also smart enough to support Manchester United so we definitely had to be friends. That's how I became friends with Mr Mdu Menze.

As a university student, when I needed help I knew I could call Mdu and I would be sorted. As we spoke more about our aspirations we realised we had more in common than football. We shared a deep passion for youth development. That is how the award-winning Waumbe Youth Development was born. This man is a hardworking machine, after work we would meet and strategise about Waumbe for long hours. I would be insanely tired and go straight to bed but Mdu would go for prayers. While I would still be sleeping he would be up running 50km as though he is being chased.

His heart is to see people transformed. I take my hat off to this great leader of our generation. He has conquered such a difficult past to be a renowned leader. I have never felt like a Zimbabwean with Mdu. I have become part of his beautiful family and he is part of mine. Together we are building the youth of Africa one individual at a time.

Aluta continua my Brother, thank you for being a great big brother. I love you.

Tshikani Mhelembe (TK), running manager, Team Just Run west coast leader

I met Mdumiseni Menze in 2017 when he visited our running group. I introduced myself and he told me who he was and everything he was and everything I needed to know. In the same year I started to notice he has potential after he completed the Soweto Marathon in 3:19. He is very humble and down to earth, he listens and is always eager to learn. He started to get proper training and eventually improved. He has been getting sub 3 since February 2018. Unfortunately he was in a car accident that year. To show that he is talented he still managed to finish his first Comrades Marathon in 7:29, without major training from an injury. With his talent, listening skills, dedication and eagerness to learn, as well as proper management, he can go far.

What I also like about him is his desire to assist needy people. There are a few events where he donated basic needs. He is a team player and he always avails himself when we need him (be it seconding other runners, or any form of contribution in the group). We are blessed to have someone of his calibre. May the great Lord continue blessing him abundantly.

www.ingramcontent.com/pod-product-compliance
Lightning Source LLC
Chambersburg PA
CBHW022109090426
42743CB00008B/776